CM Cookbook
Let's Get Cooking!

CONTINENTAL MILLS
COOKBOOK

Volume One

First Edition
Copyright © 2013 Continental Mills

Cover Design: Erica McCaig
Interior Design: Erica & Colin McCaig
Editors: Dana Ross, Rachyl Miller, Shelley Vanderpoel, Val Thorson

All rights reserved.

No part of this book may be reproduced in any form or by any electronic or mechanical means, including information storage and retrieval systems, without permission in writing from Continental Mills.

Print and color management by iocolor, Seattle
Printed in China

Food plays a lead role in so many of the moments that make up our lives. Food engages all our senses, provides comfort, and works as a vehicle for bringing friends and family together.

Food also plays both a fundamental and heroic role in our society.

Fundamental, in that it is as necessary to sustaining life as oxygen. **Heroic,** in that the food products we offer play a lead role in so many of the moments that make up our lives.

As a family owned food business, we never lose sight of the honor and responsibility that comes with providing the products that bring friends, families and communities together.

The Continental Mills Cookbook is an amazing collection of the recipes and stories from the people that make our company great.

Thank you for being part of our mission to *'Enhance People's Lives Through the Power of Food.'* All proceeds of the CM Cookbook will benefit food banks in the communities where we operate.

I hope you enjoy the great recipes and stories and share them with your family and friends!

Let's Get Cooking!

Andy Heily

All proceeds from The Continental Mills Cookbook will benefit the following charitable organizations in our communities:

Food Lifeline
Seattle, Washington
www.FoodLifeline.org

Food Lifeline feeds hungry people. We stock the shelves and fill the tables of 276 food banks, meal programs and shelters throughout Western Washington. The 35 million pounds of nutritious food we secure from restaurants, grocery stores, farmers and manufacturers feeds 745,000 of our hungry neighbors every year.

As individuals, charities, businesses and government, we all have a role to play in making sure every family has enough to eat. Support Food Lifeline. Donate. Volunteer. Advocate. Educate. Together we can solve hunger.

Flint Hills Breadbasket

A Community Food Network

Manhattan, Kansas

www.breadbasket.manhattanks.org

Mission: To minimize hunger and poverty through the distribution of available food and to nurture projects that will help alleviate hunger and poverty.

The Breadbasket's ultimate goal is to enable their clients to gain the skills necessary for self-sufficiency, and offer programs to aid this process including an Emergency Food Pantry, USDA Commodity Distribution Program, Kid's Backpack Meal Program and a Community Resource Referral Program.

Aaron McNeil House

Hopkinsville, Kentucky

www.aaronmcneil.org

"In every crisis lies the seed for opportunity." - *Author Unknown*

We are first and foremost a "Crisis Relief Center" serving all Christian County residents in need. We offer Jobs for Life classes and quarterly Budget Counseling classes.

We are dedicated to serve our community and offer services including Rental/Mortgage Payment Assistance, Electric/Gas/Water Payment Assistance, Medication Assistance, Food Pantry (We are a Feeding America Agency) and we also advocate for our clients and make referrals to other agencies.

In 1983, the Aaron McNeil House was designated a Kentucky Landmark.

Appetizers

P. 15

Soups

P. 35

Salads

P. 49

CATEGORIES

Main Dishes

P. 71

Side Dishes

P. 139

Desserts

P. 161

Etcetera!

P. 223

TABLE OF CONTENTS

APPETIZERS 15

"The Other Reason I Keep Her Around" Guacamole	17
Masala Fries	19
Family Favorite Fried Wontons	21
Chili Meatballs	23
Sausage Stars	25
Cowboy Caviar	27
Mini Corn Dogs	29
Sweet Dogs	31
Baked Fontina	33

SOUPS 35

Pelmeni	37
Bob's Chilly Hilly Chili	39
Clam Chowder New England Style	41
Curry Chicken Soup	43
Burgoo	45
Dad's Special Tomato Beef Stew	47

SALADS 49

Edamame Chopped Salad	51
Crowd Pleasing Taco Salad	53
Pasta Salad	55
Mai Fun Chicken Salad	57
Caroline's "Orange Stuff"	59
Cathy's Favorite Potato Salad	61
Layered Lettuce Salad	63
Grandma Spathelf's Summer Pasta Salad	65
Grandma Marcusen's Festive Fruit Salad	67
Summer Picnic Cooked Potato Salad	69

MAIN DISHES 71

Yorkshire Crust Pizza	73
Dorie's Chicken Afritada	75
Pulled Pork Sliders	77
Quick Chicken Pie	79
Whoa Mama Mac & Cheese	81
Heavenly Chicken Strips	83
Chicken and Cheese Enchiladas	85
Cedar Plank Grilled Salmon	87
Coconut Rice	89
Barbecue on a Stick	91
Sudado de Pescado	93
Grandpa Maher's Pigs Feet	95
Penne Pasta with Smoked Sausage and Roasted Tomatoes	97
Italian Meatballs	99
Mark's Meatloaf	101
Piroshky	103
Grandma Puderbaugh's Midwest Salisbury Steak	105
Smoked Baby Back Ribs	107
Chicken with Pears and Port	109
Down Home Hearty Golash	111
Mama's Special Sunday Fried Chicken	113
Chicken and Dumplings	115
Beans Dear Beans	117
Nasi Goreng	119
Beer Pork Roast	121
Turkey Tetrazzini	123
Lasagna by Susie	125
Chicken Imperial	127
Oven Baked Chicken	129
Simple Baked Salmon	131
Moroccan Style Lamb Roast	133
Great Gramma's Bacon Noodles	135
Easy Pasta with Shrimp	137

SIDE DISHES — 139

Amina's Spicy Potatoes	141
Green Bean Bundles	143
Twice as Nice Baked Potatoes	145
Mexican Elote	147
Verda's Baked Beans	149
Jerusalem Green Beans	151
Smashed Potato Gratin	153
Mom's "Everyone's Together" Broccoli & Rice Casserole	155
Roasted Butternut Squash	157
Zucchini Bake	159

DESSERTS — 161

Red and White Layered Raspberry Pie	163
'Grand Champion' Sugar Cookies	165
Nana's Thumbprint Cookies	167
Mom's Chocolate Fudge	169
Dorie's Leche Flan	171
Sopapilla Cheesecake Bars	173
Summer Time Ice Cream Treat	175
Apple Crunch	177
Grandma Nita's Chocolate Dessert	179
Chocolate Peanut Butter No Bake Cookies	181
Fresh Strawberry Pie	183
Chocolate Cake with Maple Frosting	185
Linda's Apple Pie	187
Pot O'Dirt	189
Monster Cookies	191
Blueberry Bread Pudding	193
Grandma Caroline's Pfeffernuesse	195
Cookie Grammy's Famous Chocolate Cake with Peanut Butter Frosting	197
Chocolate Mousse	199
Beulah Mae's Old Fashioned Banana Pudding	201
Southern Pecan Pie	203
Little Mama's Fruit Cake Recipe	205
Grandma Puderbaugh's Peanut Butter Fudge	207
Linda's Cheesecake	209
Danish Almond Puff	211
Wonderful Lemon Cake	213
Soft Chocolate Chip Cookies	215
Great Grandma Vi's World War I Cake	217
Norwegian Krumkake	219
Strawberry Danish Delight	221

ETCETERA — 223

Johnny's Secret Sauce	225
Hot Fudge Sauce	227
Doughnuts	229
Twistree Bread	231
Grandad's Best Popovers	233
Better Than Grandma's Yeast Rolls	235
Grama's Old Fashioned Graham Bread	237
Breakfast Bars	239
Blueberry Smoothie Recipe	241
Award-Winning Gourmet Cinnamon Rolls	243
Grandma's Cherry Coffee Cake	245
Orpha's Sour Cream Donuts	247
Banana & Coconut Pudding Shots	249

ACKNOWLEDGEMENTS — 251

CONVERSION TABLE — 252

APPETIZERS

APPETIZERS

Every time we entertain in the summer, my husband always asks that I make this guacamole. **According to him, it's the best guacamole he's ever tasted and he brags about it non-stop to our friends.**

His favorite saying whenever I serve it is ***"this is the other reason I keep her around".*** He has said this so many times over the years that now all of our friends repeat this whenever I bring it out to the table. Whenever our friends entertain and are serving Mexican food, I always get asked to make it.

After all these years, it's funny that no one has ever asked him what is the *first reason* he keeps me around!

LEESA TUCKER

"THE OTHER REASON I KEEP HER AROUND"
GUACAMOLE

INGREDIENTS

½ medium white onion, chopped and rinsed

3 plum tomatoes, seeded and chopped

¼ cup fresh cilantro

3-4 medium-large ripe avocados

2-3 tablespoons lime juice (or to taste)

¼ teaspoon kosher salt (or to taste)

2-3 jalapenos (or to taste)

INSTRUCTIONS

Roast the chilies in a small ungreased skillet set over medium heat. Turn them every minute until softened and the skin is blistered. Chop them into a small dice and then place in a large bowl.

Place the chopped onion into a small strainer and rinse under cold water and shake off excess water. Add the tomatoes and cilantro to the bowl with the onion.

Cut each avocado in half and take out the pits. Scoop out the avocado into the bowl and then mash with a potato masher until some of the avocado is mashed, but you want to leave some chunks.

Season the guacamole with the kosher salt and lemon juice to taste. It's best to add a little at a time until it's seasoned to your preference.

Serve with good quality corn tortilla chips.

PEOPLE SERVED: 6

APPETIZERS

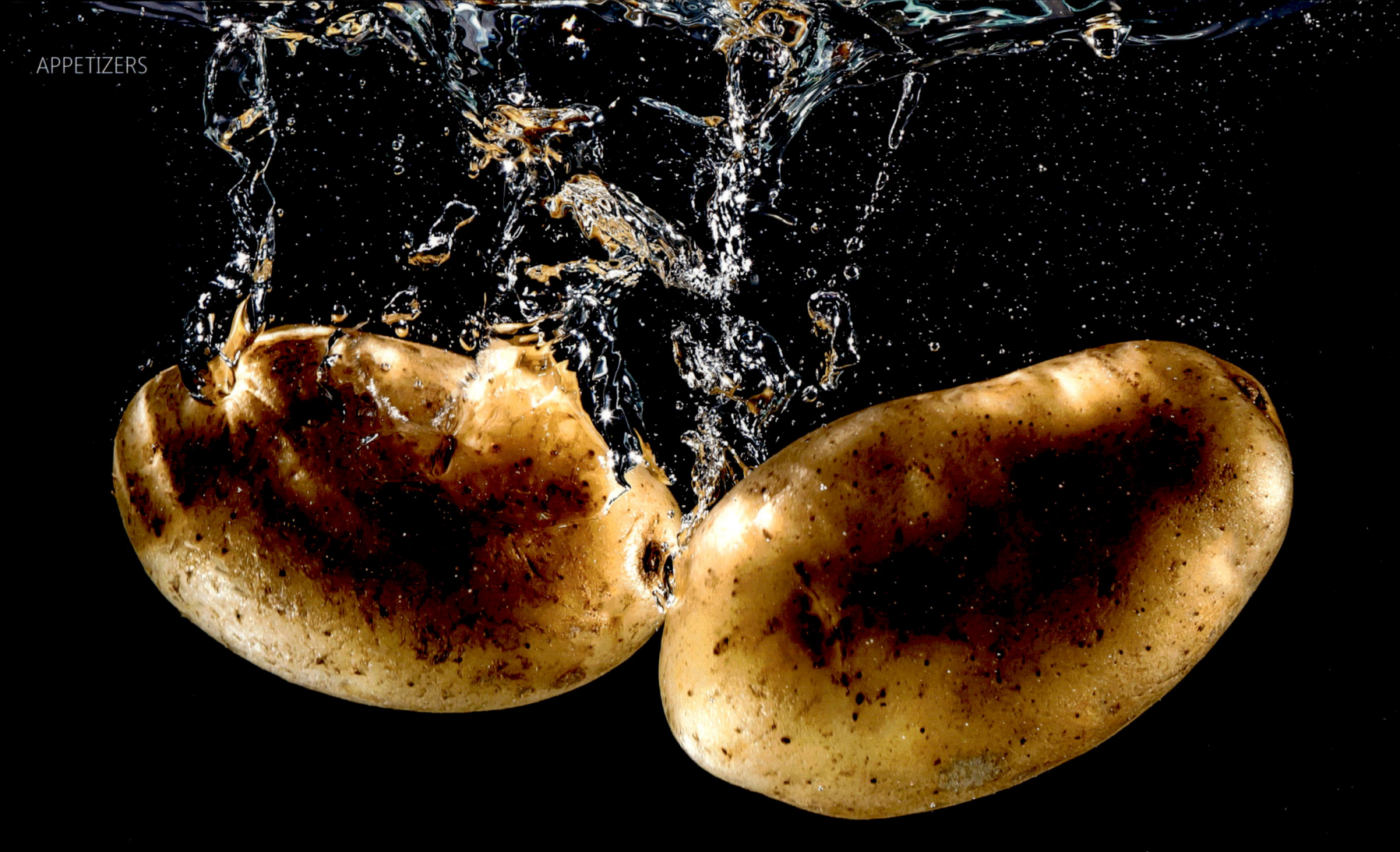

Growing up, we always had a treat with our afternoon chai on weekends.

My mom would make a hot, spicy, fresh treat to go along with the spiced tea for everyone!

It was anything from samosas to pakodas to masala fries.

MASALA FRIES

INGREDIENTS

4 large russet potatoes, peeled and cut into ¼ inch fingers

1 quart vegetable oil, for frying

Masala Seasoning:

1 teaspoon chili powder

½ teaspoon cumin powder

¼ teaspoon black salt

¼ teaspoon kosher salt

1 lemon, cut into wedges

ADDITIONAL NOTES

For a healthier version, you can bake the fries before adding the seasoning!

INSTRUCTIONS

Parboil the potato fingers in salted water for 5-7 minutes. Drain the water and let the potatoes cool on a paper towel.

In a large pan, heat oil over medium heat.

Deep fry the potato fingers in hot oil until they turn golden brown. Carefully remove the fries from the oil and set aside to drain on paper towel.

Mix together the chili powder, cumin powder, black salt and kosher salt for the masala seasoning.

Sprinkle the masala seasoning on the fries and toss until the fries are well coated.

Serve hot with lemon wedges.

PEOPLE SERVED: 4

Potato fries are one of the most popular snacks, appetizers or sides with a meal in nearly every part of the world, in some form or other.

Here is a simple recipe to transform your regular fries into a spiced delight!

LAVANYA VENKATESWAR

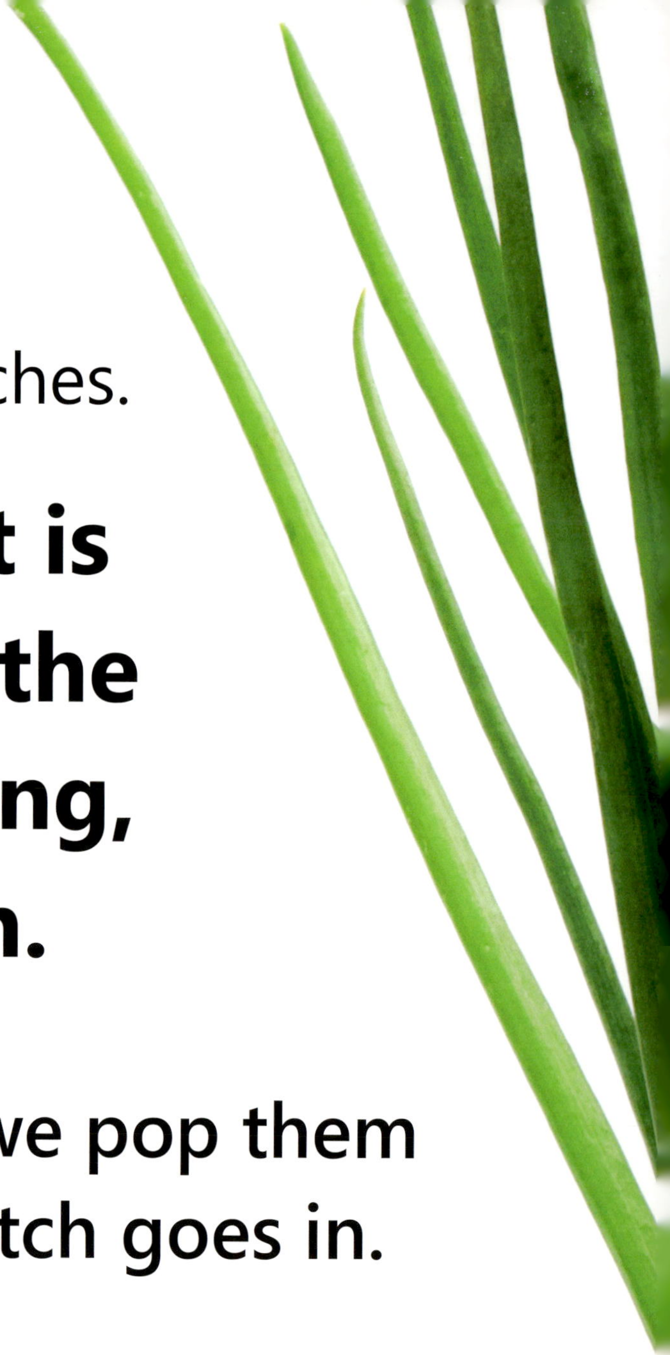

APPETIZERS

I fry these up for my family in batches.

The most enjoyable part is the time we all spend in the kitchen as these are frying, waiting in anticipation.

When the first ones are ready, we pop them in our mouths and the next batch goes in.

I keep frying until we've all had our fill.

LISA EVENSON

FAMILY FAVORITE
FRIED WONTONS

INGREDIENTS

1 pound ground pork

3 green onions, finely chopped

1 clove garlic, crushed

1 egg

1 tablespoon soy sauce

1 tablespoon sesame seeds

1 package wonton wrappers (about 50 sheets)

Oil for frying

INSTRUCTIONS

Combine pork, green onions, garlic, egg, soy sauce, and sesame seeds.

Fill wontons by laying wrappers on a flat work surface and lightly moistening all four edges with water.

Place about 1 teaspoonful pork mixture in center of each wonton wrapper. Fold wonton wrapper over filling to form a triangle. Turn top of triangle down toward fold. Turn over and press corners together.

Deep fry wontons in hot oil until golden brown, about 4-5 minutes or until done.

Drain on paper towels and serve with your favorite dipping sauce.

PEOPLE SERVED: 6-8

APPETIZERS

We never had a family celebration without a crockpot full of meatballs and hotdogs **in an amazing sauce that was a closely guarded family secret**... People could drop by all day and the meatballs would just get better and better.

After I moved away and started making these at my own get-togethers I would ask friends to guess what ingredients were in the meatballs.

Imagine my surprise when one person after another would guess correctly.

Turns out that my family secret recipe was just that for a lot of other families too!

STACI SMITH

CHILI MEATBALLS

INGREDIENTS

3 pounds frozen meatballs

1 package hot dogs or little smokies

32 ounce jar grape jelly

2 - 12 ounce jars Heinz chili sauce

PEOPLE SERVED: 10

INSTRUCTIONS

Mix the grape jelly and chili sauce in a crockpot or sauce pan. Heat slowly while stirring to combine. Add frozen meatballs and sliced hotdogs. Heat through and serve warm.

This turns out even better if you take the time to oven brown the meatballs and pan fry the hot dog slices before adding them to the sauce.

SAUSAGE STARS

INGREDIENTS

One pack wonton wraps
(found in the produce department)

2 tubes breakfast sausage

2 green onions, chopped finely

1 - 8 ounce package finely shredded cheese
(I use cheddar, but you can use any kind)

1 small can chopped black olives

1 - 6 ounce tub sour cream

1 package powdered ranch dressing mix

PEOPLE SERVED: 10

INSTRUCTIONS

Preheat oven to 350°F.

Cook sausage as normal and drain.

Prepare ranch dressing mix as directed with the sour cream and chill in the fridge.

Brush a light amount of vegetable oil on each side of the wonton wraps and set in cupcake tray, pushing the wraps down into the tray to form a cup or star shape. Put in oven for 5 to 7 minutes or until lightly golden. Do not darken too much. Let them cool for a few minutes. You can remove them from the tray if needed. They should be hard enough to hold their shape.

Mix onions, olives, about half your bag of cheese, sausage and ranch in a bowl.

Place the star shells back into the cupcake tray and spoon desired amount of mixture into the stars and top with cheese. Put back into the oven for 5 minutes or until cheese is melted on top.

These amounts should make about 36-40 stars generously filled. I found that if you fill them moderately, you can make 10-15 more. It all depends on how much of the filling you want in the wonton wraps. I have also substituted the sausage with ground beef and they were delicious also.

I've been serving these for years: my family and friends have always enjoyed them!

BRIAN SMITH

Cowboy Caviar is a family favorite that we always serve at our Kansas State Football Tailgates.

Sometimes I add a little more jalapeno for an extra **kick!**

LORI VILKANSKAS

COWBOY CAVIAR

INGREDIENTS

2 cups shoepeg corn, drained

2 cups black beans, drained

6 green onions, chopped

½ purple onion, chopped

1 jalapeno, chopped

4 tablespoons fresh cilantro, chopped

4 roma tomatoes, chopped

½ cup Wishbone sweet & spicy French salad dressing

½ cup Italian salad dressing

INSTRUCTIONS

Mix it all together and marinate (overnight if possible).

Serve with tortilla chips.

PEOPLE SERVED: 15

APPETIZERS

This was my kids favorite way to eat hot dogs.

DONNA AKIN

MINI CORN DOGS

INGREDIENTS

⅓ cup cornmeal

½ cup flour

¾ teaspoon salt

¾ teaspoon baking powder

2 ½ teaspoons sugar

⅓ cup milk

1 egg beaten

½ pound hot dogs (cut into thirds)

INSTRUCTIONS

Mix first 5 ingredients.

Add milk and egg. Dip hot dogs in mixture and fry in hot oil.

Note: I use a toothpick in the middle of each hot dog and dip in oil.

PEOPLE SERVED: 4

APPETIZERS

My Aunt Mary Ellen made these for a holiday party at her house and I loved them so I asked for the recipe to try my hand at it.

Good for tailgating events or sporting event parties.

CINDY FULLER

SWEET DOGS

INGREDIENTS

1 package hot dogs

1 package bacon

3 cups brown sugar

PEOPLE SERVED: 8 -10

INSTRUCTIONS

Cut your hot dogs in three pieces, cut your bacon in half, then wrap the bacon around the hot dog and put a toothpick through it to hold it together. Place in crock pot on low.

Then add the 3 cups of brown sugar over the hot dogs.

Cook 4 hours, stirring every hour.

APPETIZERS

This recipe is perfect with a glass of wine on a winter night!

LORI VILKANSKAS

BAKED FONTINA - EASY AND DELISH!

INGREDIENTS

1 ½ pounds Italian fontina cheese, rind removed, and cut in 1-inch dice

¼ cup good olive oil

6 garlic cloves, thinly sliced

1 tablespoon fresh thyme leaves, minced

1 teaspoon fresh rosemary leaves, minced

1 teaspoon kosher salt

1 teaspoon freshly ground black pepper

1 crusty French baguette

INSTRUCTIONS

Preheat the broiler and position the oven rack 5 inches from the heat.

Distribute the cubes of fontina evenly in a 12-inch cast-iron pan. Drizzle on the olive oil. Combine the garlic, thyme, and rosemary and sprinkle it over the cheese and olive oil. Sprinkle with the salt and pepper and place the pan under the broiler for 6 minutes until the cheese is melted and bubbling and starts to brown.

Serve the Baked Fontina family-style, right out of the oven in the cast-iron pan with crusty chunks of bread for everyone to dip.

PEOPLE SERVED: 6

SOUPS

SOUPS

Pelmeni took time for my Russian grandmother to make a thousand of these for five boys, but on a cold winter day I can see myself in the Doctor Zhivago movie.

My grandmother and mom inspired me to fake numerous illnesses to miss school and stay home to watch the Galloping Gourmet, Graham Kerr, sans wine.

I will always remember those Russian dishes and the accumulated family history behind them.

I am pretty sure after 4 years of Top Ramen in college, **my kids might long for a hot bowl of Pelmeni!**

PELMENI

INGREDIENTS

1 ½ cups flour

2 eggs

½ cup water

½ teaspoon salt

½ pound ground beef

½ pound ground pork

2 medium onions, finely chopped

1 teaspoon salt

½ teaspoon black pepper

Garlic to taste

INSTRUCTIONS

To make the dough, combine the flour, eggs, water and ½ teaspoon salt. Knead mixture. Let rest for 30 minutes.

Mix the ground beef, ground pork, onions, 1 teaspoon salt, pepper and garlic together.

Cut the dough into three equally sized pieces and roll each one into a cylinder the diameter of a finger. Cut each cylinder into pieces the size of a walnut, and then roll each piece into a very thin flat cake with a diameter of about 2 inches.

Put some of the ground meat mixture in the center of each flat cake (quite a lot, but not so much that you can't then seal up the dough). Then fold the dough in half and join up the edges to seal them. Pinch the corners together: you should now have a ravioli-shaped "flying saucer."

Boil the Pelmeni in salted water for seven minutes or until they float to the surface.

Serve in soup bowls with some of the cooking broth. I like to offer three dipping sauces: sour cream, creamy horseradish, and white wine vinegar.

PEOPLE SERVED: 4

Sitting in my recipe box on a crumpled white index card is a hand written chili recipe. My family calls it "Bob's Chili" **named after a dear family friend who first served this chili to us when I was about 5 years old.**

Bob is a longtime friend of my parents. He was a professor at WSU in Pullman where I grew up, and a customer at my dad's 2-chair barber shop on campus. As a little girl, I would draw pictures for "Uncle Bob" and he would proudly display my art work on his walls.

Years later Bob moved to Bainbridge Island, which happens to be the location of the first organized bike ride of the season in the Seattle area called "Chilly Hilly".

My husband and I would take part in this ride and "Uncle Bob" would invite us to his home after the ride and serve us and our friends his chili

– *now named…*

"Bob's Chilly Hilly Chili."

JUDY ELSE

BOB'S CHILLY HILLY CHILI

INGREDIENTS

1 pound extra lean ground beef

1 large onion, diced

1 - 16 ounce can dark red kidney beans

1 - 30 ounce can tomatoes, cut up

2 tablespoons mild chili powder

2 tablespoons sugar

3 tablespoons white vinegar

1 cup ketchup

1 teaspoon salt or adjust to taste

½ teaspoon pepper or adjust to taste

INSTRUCTIONS

In a large sauce pan, brown ground beef. Add other ingredients. Bring to a bubbling boil.

Reduce heat and simmer for 45 minutes, stirring occasionally.

Can also be made in a crock pot.

PEOPLE SERVED: 6

SOUPS

In my family, weekends with extra low tides meant camping out and clam digging at the ocean or Hood Canal.

We steamed up the butter clams and fried the razor clams.

If the digging was good my grandmother would have enough to put through the meat grinder and can up a batch to use later for chowder or clam fritters.

Today my clams come from the grocery store, but I always think about those fun days when I make a batch of chowder.

BOBBI MILLER

CLAM CHOWDER NEW ENGLAND STYLE

INGREDIENTS

2 to 3 slices thick cut bacon, cut crosswise into ¼ inch strips

3 tablespoons butter

1 large yellow onion, cut into small dice (about 2 cups)

4 tender inner celery stalks, cut into ⅓ inch dice (about 1 cup)

4 - 6.5 ounce cans chopped clams (drain the juice from the cans and reserve)

16 ounce canned or bottled clam juice (combine with reserved clam juice to make about 4 cups clam nectar)

2 pounds large Yukon gold potatoes, peeled and cut into ½-inch dice (about 4 ½ cups)

1 teaspoon chopped fresh thyme

Freshly ground pepper

1 cup heavy cream

3 tablespoons chopped fresh flat-leaf parsley

Kosher salt

INSTRUCTIONS

Cook the bacon in a wide heavy-duty 4-5 quart pot or Dutch oven over medium heat, stirring occasionally, until just beginning to turn crisp and golden, about 4 minutes.

Remove from heat. Pour off and discard bacon fat, leaving bacon in the pot. Add butter and onion and cook over low heat, covered, stirring occasionally, until onion is softened but not colored, about 8 minutes.

Add celery and cook, uncovered, stirring occasionally, until just softened, about 5 minutes.

Add clam juice, potatoes, thyme, and 1 teaspoon pepper. Bring to a boil over high heat. Lower the heat to maintain a simmer and cook, partially covered, until potatoes are tender, 10 to 12 minutes.

Puree 1 cup of the soup solids with just enough liquid to cover in a food processor or blender, or by mashing in a bowl, and add it back to the soup. Add cream and bring to a boil.

Remove soup from heat, wait until it stops simmering, and stir in clams and parsley. Season to taste with salt and pepper.

PEOPLE SERVED: 8

This is one of the few actual recipes I have written out.

I usually cook from memory and create from there. I have had so many requests for this soup that I finally typed it up.

Enjoy!

TIM ST. PETER

CURRY CHICKEN SOUP

INGREDIENTS

1 ½ pounds chicken breast, skinless/cubed

1 cup chicken stock

2 tablespoons canola oil

1 sweet onion, sliced/chopped/etc.

1 red and yellow bell pepper, sliced

1 red apple, peeled/diced

3-4 cloves garlic, chopped

4 tablespoons hoisin sauce (or to taste)

2 tablespoons red curry paste

1 tablespoon yellow curry powder & turmeric

2 cans coconut milk

1 tablespoon apricot preserve (it's okay to sub peach/plum/etc.)

Adding asparagus and/or cilantro is optional

PEOPLE SERVED: 6 (OR 3 MAINTENANCE TECHS)

INSTRUCTIONS

Spread cubed chicken out on plate/sheet pan and dust with yellow curry powder and turmeric.

Add chicken to medium sauce pan with pre-heated canola oil. Remove chicken after all sides are seared. This may take 2 batches as you don't want to overfill the pan with chicken as it cools the pan down too fast.

Add onion to the pan and the red curry paste. Let this cook down about two minutes and then add garlic. Stir for approximately one minute and then add chicken stock, bell peppers, hoisin sauce & fruit preserve.

Add back the chicken and then turn heat down to medium-low before adding the coconut milk. Let cook for 10-15 minutes and then taste for salt & spice. Adjust with red curry & hoisin sauce if needed until you get it right. Some sea salt won't hurt either.

I like to add the asparagus & apples for the last five minutes of cooking. I hate to over-cook these.

This is great with a Grilled Pineapple Salad.

Try it out.

SOUPS

Burgoo is something that I have found to be **unique to the state of Kentucky.**

I first remember trying it when I was a kid.

As a lover of both BBQ and vegetable soup, I was won over immediately.

It's perfect for a meal or a late night snack.

STEFAN P'POOL

BURGOO

INGREDIENTS

1 pound cooked BBQ boston butt

1 cooked BBQ chicken

1 pound cooked BBQ ribs

1 large onion

2 large garlic cloves

2 - 15 ounce cans lima beans

2 - 14.5 ounce cans green beans

2 - 15.25 ounce cans black-eyed peas

2 - 14.5 ounce cans green peas

2 - 14.5 ounce cans sliced carrots

2 - 15.25 ounce cans whole kernel corn

2 cups cooked cabbage or canned

1 - 16 ounce package frozen okra (optional)

3 cups cubed potatoes

1 - 46 ounce can or bottle original V8 Juice

2 - 15 ounce cans tomato puree

1 - 13 ounce bottle ketchup

¼ cup sugar

2 tablespoons vinegar

½ teaspoon cloves

¼ cup steak sauce

⅓ cup Worcestershire sauce

½ cup Tabasco sauce

¾ to 1 teaspoon red pepper flakes

1 ½ to 2 teaspoons black pepper

Salt to taste

PEOPLE SERVED: A MESS

INSTRUCTIONS

Chop BBQ meats, onion and garlic. Add to cubed potatoes in a 12 quart stock pot. Add about 6 cups of water and cook until potatoes are tender, about 30 minutes.

When potatoes are tender add all remaining ingredients.

Cook over medium heat about 3 hours, stirring often so it doesn't stick to the bottom of the pot.

If it's not hot enough for ya, adjust the Tabasco sauce, red pepper flakes and black pepper to your taste.

SOUPS

Other than grilling, my dad only cooked one or two things.

His Tomato Beef Stew is one of my favorite comfort foods to this day. The ingredients usually used fresh root vegetables of a wide variety. **The stew would cook on the stove during the day and it smelled so good that by the time dinner was served,**
boy were we ready!

Red Lobster Cheddar Bay Biscuits would be an excellent accompaniment...

RAYE RAPP

DAD'S SPECIAL TOMATO BEEF STEW

INGREDIENTS

2 pounds beef stew meat

⅛ cup flour

2 tablespoons vegetable oil

2 teaspoons salt

1 tablespoon fresh ground pepper

2 large cloves garlic, minced

2 large onions, chopped

1 - 18 ounce can stewed tomatoes with juice

1 - 18 ounce can tomato sauce

8 ounce beef broth

5 potatoes cut into quarters (use russets, purple, red, whatever you want)

10 carrots peeled and cut into large chunks, then halved lengthwise

2 sticks celery, chopped

1 large turnip, chopped

1 large parsnip, chopped (you can add sweet potatoes or any other root veggie as well)

½ teaspoon dried thyme or Italian seasoning (add some rosemary if you want as well)

1 bay leaf (remove before serving)

INSTRUCTIONS

On medium-high heat, add the vegetable oil to a large heavy pot (one that has a tight fitting lid).

Put flour in a baggie and add the stew meat and shake to coat the meat.

When oil begins to smoke slightly, add the beef and brown very well. Do in batches if necessary. Add the salt and pepper as the beef browns.

Once browned, remove the beef with a slotted spoon, set aside. Add the onions, garlic and a little more oil, sauté for about 5 minutes, until softened.

Add the stewed tomatoes and stir to deglaze. Add the tomato sauce, beef broth, meat, and all the veggies.

Add the spices and simmer for at least 2 hours, until the veggies are tender.

Taste and add a little A1 Steak Sauce or Worcestershire sauce for a little kick.

PEOPLE SERVED: 8

SALADS

SALADS

This is a fast and easy salad for potlucks, summer picnics, etc.

It transports very well.

Throw in some chopped chicken or salami and it can become lunch. If you are missing one of the vegetable ingredients, substitute something else.

Very versatile and easy to prepare, especially if the potluck is tomorrow and you don't know what to bring.

JEAN GREEN

EDAMAME CHOPPED SALAD

INGREDIENTS

1 red or orange bell pepper, seeded and coarsely chopped

⅓ cup finely diced sweet onion

12 ounces edamame, either frozen and prepared or canned and rinsed

2 cups sliced zucchini

⅓ cup Italian salad dressing, add more as needed (½ cup is plenty)

2 tablespoons Mediterranean pesto or finely diced olives

INSTRUCTIONS

Mix all ingredients together in medium bowl. Refrigerate until needed.

Stir again just before serving.

PEOPLE SERVED: 8-10

SALADS

My sister came up with this recipe. One thing our mom let us do was experiment in the kitchen.

Some experiments came out awesome: others the dog would not eat.

It has always been fun telling folks they were eating an experiment. The look on their face is priceless. This method is how we could tell if the experiment was a hit or miss.

I have used this recipe for many functions that I have attended over the years. **Everybody that has tasted this dish has wanted the recipe.** It is very simple to make and it is a crowd pleaser.

JOANN GREEN

CROWD PLEASING
TACO SALAD

INGREDIENTS

1 - 31 ounce can refried beans

2 pounds ground chuck, browned and drained

1 - 1.5 ounce package taco seasoning

1 - 16 ounce jar salsa

4 cups fiesta cheese, separated into 2 cup portions

1 - 8 ounce bag shredded lettuce

6 small roma tomatoes, diced

1 - 16 ounce container sour cream

2 bags tortilla chips for dipping

INSTRUCTIONS

Brown ground chuck and drain.

Add taco seasoning to ground chuck, let simmer 5 minutes (do not add water).

Layer in 13X9-inch pan as follows:

Refried beans, seasoned ground chuck, salsa, 2 cups fiesta cheese, shredded lettuce, roma tomatoes, 2 cups fiesta cheese.

Lastly, using a large tablespoon, spoon sour cream on top (do not spread).

PEOPLE SERVED: 10-15

My mom made this one night for dinner. My dad and I sat at the table talking and eating. The next thing we realized, we had eaten the whole bowl!

My mother and brother didn't have a chance to try it.

So, every time she makes this salad she makes two portions; one for my dad and me, and one for everyone else.

Enjoy!

SCOTT BURNETT

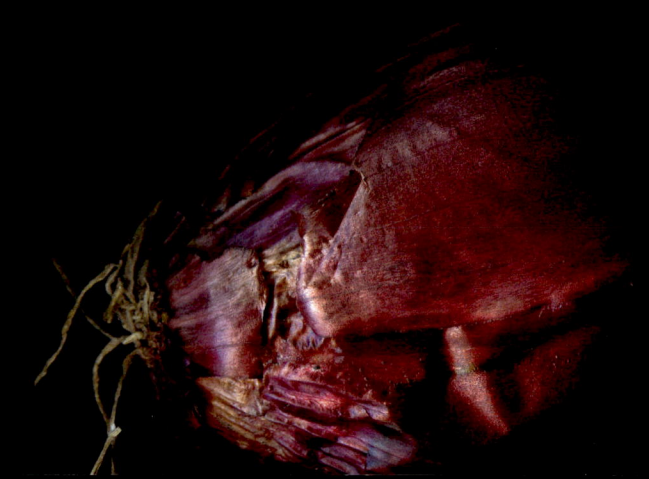

PASTA SALAD

INGREDIENTS

16 ounce box rotini pasta (spiral)

1 small package cherry tomatoes

1 bag broccoli florets

1 red onion

1 English cucumber

3 tablespoons salad seasoning

16 ounce bottle Italian dressing

INSTRUCTIONS

Cook the pasta, drain in cold water.

Quarter the cherry tomatoes. Cut the florets in half or thirds.

Slice up the onion into rings then quarter them. Cut up cucumber into slices, then in half.

Add pasta and vegetables into a mixing bowl, mix together. Add 4 ounces of the dressing, mix well.

Sprinkle salad seasoning over the salad, and mix.

Add more dressing or seasoning to your desired taste.

PEOPLE SERVED: 6-8

SALADS

Every year growing up my family had the tradition of going to Sunriver, Oregon.

Sunriver was a place you could park the car for the week and ride your bike everywhere – to town, the pool and marina were some of our favorite places! It is about a 6 hour drive to Sunriver, so my parents would prepare the ingredients for **"Sunriver Special"** the night before we left for our trip, and then we'd leave early the next morning. Once we arrived, all we had to do was toss everything together and enjoy!

Nowadays we don't always make it down to Sunriver each year, **but we sometimes make "Sunriver Special" during the summertime and reminisce about the many fond memories.**

TARA BUNKER

MAI FUN CHICKEN SALAD
A.K.A. SUNRIVER SPECIAL

INGREDIENTS

3 chicken breasts, deboned

7 slices fresh ginger

1 head cabbage, shredded (or lettuce)

3 ounces dry ramen noodles, crumbled

1 bunch green onions, chopped (or to taste)

¼ cup sesame seeds, toasted

½ cup sliced almonds, toasted

Dressing:

4 tablespoons sugar

1 teaspoon salt

½ teaspoon pepper

4 tablespoons white vinegar

2 tablespoons rice vinegar

Minced ginger (from above)

½ cup oil

⅛ cup olive oil

INSTRUCTIONS

Boil large pot of water. Once boiling, add chicken breasts and fresh ginger and cook for 20-28 minutes while covered.

Remove chicken from water and save ginger for dressing. Place in refrigerator overnight, or until cool. After cooled, shred the chicken.

For dressing, in a frying pan combine sugar, salt, pepper, white vinegar, rice vinegar and ginger over low heat and dissolve. Remove from heat and let cool. Add oil and olive oil.

Toss all ingredients when ready to eat. Travels well, as the dressing waits until serving time.

PEOPLE SERVED: 4-6

SALADS

This recipe, courtesy of my stepmother Caroline, has been a family favorite for many years.

No holiday meal is ever considered complete without the Orange Stuff.

Over the years we have tried multiple times to come up with a name more fitting the stature of this dish, which is sometimes a side dish, and sometimes a dessert.

We've tried out names like 'Orange Dream', 'Orange Whip Delite' & 'Orange Tapioca Surprise'. It has generated many a lively after-dinner discussion, but nothing has stuck like the original Orange Stuff.

Whatever it is, it'll go down in Barr family history as one of the most asked-for dishes ever!

TAMMY BARR

CAROLINE'S "ORANGE STUFF"

INGREDIENTS

6 cups water, boiling

2 packages orange Jell-O

2 packages tapioca pudding mix (not instant)

2 packages vanilla pudding mix (not instant)

2 cups frozen whipped cream topping, thawed

2 - 6 ounce cans mandarin orange sections

INSTRUCTIONS

Add Jell-O and puddings to boiling water. Stir for 5 minutes. Take off heat and cool in cold water. When cool, mix in thawed whipped topping and oranges.

Refrigerate until firm.

PEOPLE SERVED: 12

SALADS

I will always remember my mother as being a very good cook.

She made mouth-watering roasts out of the lesser expensive cuts of meats. Her gravies were always perfectly seasoned and contained zero lumps.

And, her bread making abilities were amazing.

Regretfully, I never learned how to match her skills when it came to perfecting the basics of making perfect gravy, mouth-watering breads, and pot roasts that seemed to melt in your mouth.

After trying several different potato salad recipes and not finding one that I was in love with, **I realized that I was going to have to create my own recipe if I were to ever become a lover of potato salad.**

So, I experimented by combining the certain attributes I liked, from a variety of potato salad recipes, into what is termed by my family and friends, as

"Cathy's Potato Salad."

CATHY MONTPLAISIR

CATHY'S FAVORITE POTATO SALAD

INGREDIENTS

6 large russet potatoes

3 eggs, boiled

½ cup celery, chopped

¼ cup dill pickle, chopped

¼ cup onion, chopped (optional)

1 teaspoon salt

2 teaspoons dill weed

2 cups mayonnaise (regular or lite)

½ teaspoon mustard

Add ground black pepper to taste (optional)

Feel free to borrow and modify to fit your individual style and tastes...

PEOPLE SERVED: 6-8

INSTRUCTIONS

Clean and scrub potatoes under cool running water. Do not peel the potatoes.

Place potatoes in a large pot, add water, add a sprinkle of salt and then cover with a lid. Cook using high heat, until the water begins to boil. Then reduce heat to med-high, set the lid to the vent, and continue cooking until tender, but still slightly firm in the middle. Check potatoes for doneness, using a large fork, after about 20 minutes. Large potatoes could take up to 45 minutes to reach doneness.

Using tongs, carefully transfer each potato from the pot of hot water, placing them in a flat dish. Allow potatoes to cool, uncovered, for 15 minutes. Then lightly cover the potatoes and store in the refrigerator overnight.

Place eggs in a saucepan and cover with cold water. Bring water to boil for 1 minute; cover pot, lower heat and simmer for 10-12 minutes. Remove from heat and let rest for 20 minutes. Place pan of eggs in the sink and run cool water over the eggs to cool; crack eggs under the cool running water and remove egg shells. Dry eggs with paper towels and place in a plastic bag or covered bowl and refrigerate until ready to use.

Peel cooled potatoes with small paring knife to remove potato skins. Cut potatoes into larger bite size chunks or the potatoes may become mushy.

Clean 2 stalks of celery under cool running water. Cut off the ends and remove the tops. Then split the celery stalks lengthwise and cut into smaller strips.

Chop dill pickles into small bits, approximately ¼ cup. Chop eggs into small pieces.

Mix together mayonnaise, mustard, salt, dill weed, and pepper.

In a large bowl, combine the potatoes and seasoned mayonnaise. Mix together lightly making sure to coat the potatoes thoroughly, and then refrigerate until chilled.

SALADS

This recipe has been handed down for at least four generations.

My grandmother got it from her great aunt in Minnesota who ran an Inn. We always have it for one family gathering or another. I introduced it to my husband's family and they always request it at their gatherings now.

I plan on passing it down to my kids as well, making it 5 generations!

JANET DEBORD

LAYERED LETTUCE SALAD

INGREDIENTS

1 head lettuce

1 cup diced celery

6 hard-boiled eggs

10 ounces frozen sweet peas, raw

½ cup green pepper, diced

1 medium onion, diced

8 slices bacon, diced and fried

2 cups mayonnaise

2 tablespoons sugar

4 to 8 ounces cheddar or swiss cheese, grated

INSTRUCTIONS

Layer the first seven ingredients in the order given in a large serving bowl. Mix the mayonnaise and sugar until the sugar is dissolved. Spread it over the layered ingredients like frosting on top. Sprinkle the grated cheese over the top.

Chilling overnight gives the best flavor, but can be chilled for a few hours. Toss salad well before serving.

Variations: Use mixed salad greens, add diced chicken or ham, add tomatoes, green onions, radishes, avocado, black olives, or bleu cheese.

PEOPLE SERVED: 10-12

SALADS

This pasta salad recipe has been a staple at our family gatherings since the 1950's.

Back then, wedding receptions, graduation parties, christenings and family reunions were held at the local fire hall and everyone brought a covered dish.

This dish was always my grandmother's contribution to the buffet table and she passed the recipe down to my mom, who now brings it to our family gatherings.

It's still a big hit at family cook-outs and summer picnics.

TIFFANY LUBY

GRANDMA SPATHELF'S SUMMER PASTA SALAD

INGREDIENTS

1 ½ pounds pasta (shape of your choice)

2 tablespoons olive oil

1 pound salami

1 pound American cheese

1 pound provolone cheese

1 cup Parmesan cheese

2 - 6 ounce cans black olives, sliced

2 pints grape tomatoes, sliced in half

2 cups Italian dressing

INSTRUCTIONS

Cook pasta according to the directions on the box. Drain, add oil and toss to prevent sticking. Place in refrigerator to cool.

Place cooled pasta in an airtight container.

Dice salami and cheeses and add to pasta. Add Parmesan, sliced black olives, halved tomatoes and Italian dressing.

Mix all ingredients together and refrigerate overnight.

ADDITIONAL NOTES

For variety you can add whatever meat and cheeses your family prefers. You can also substitute with green olives.

PEOPLE SERVED: 12-15

SALADS

This was Grandma's family favorite holiday salad. We always had it at Thanksgiving, Christmas, and Easter.

It was that dish you just couldn't live without!

GRANDMA MARCUSEN'S
FESTIVE FRUIT SALAD

INGREDIENTS

1 large can sliced peaches, cut in smaller chunks

2 large cans pineapple chunks

1 medium jar maraschino cherries, whole

2 bananas, sliced

Fruit salad dressing (*below*)

Fruit Salad Dressing:

½ cup sugar

1 ½ tablespoons cornstarch

Juice drained from fruit

2 tablespoons lemon juice

2 tablespoons orange juice

INSTRUCTIONS

Fruit Salad:

Drain fruit, saving drained juice for the dressing. Combine fruit in medium sized bowl. Add cooked dressing after it has cooled. Add bananas just before serving.

Fruit Salad Dressing:

Mix sugar and cornstarch in small saucepan. Stir in reserved fruit juices. Cook, stirring constantly until mixture thickens and boils. Boil and stir 1 minute. Remove from heat. Stir in remaining ingredients and let cool.

PEOPLE SERVED: 8-10

Every time I make this salad, it brings back fond memories of my grandmother whom I was very close to. She was a wonderful cook and everything she made was from scratch.

SHELLEY VANDERPOEL

This recipe was a staple in the summer when everyone would gather for family picnics.

This was the official recipe, but my grandmother never made it quite this way; embellishing depending on what was fresh in the garden at the time.

Eventually, Grandma was not able to stand for long periods and started turning the cooking duties over to my grandfather, who took them on with his usual flair. A favorite family memory involves this potato salad…

Grandpa had made, and proudly served, the potato salad at one of our summer picnics. **Everyone began eating, and the looks around the table made it obvious something was seriously wrong.** In fact, Grandpa had forgotten to cook the potatoes, so everyone was eating a raw, barely edible, potato salad! Not wanting to hurt his feelings, we managed a few bites and were wondering what to do next.

By then, my grandfather is remembered to have said…

"you know, I think I forgot to cook the potatoes…"

The salad has since become known as the "cooked" potato salad, just so no one else forgets!

SUMMER PICNIC COOKED POTATO SALAD

INGREDIENTS

1 ¼ pounds cooked, diced potatoes (3 ½ cups)

2 hard cooked eggs, chopped

½ cup celery, chopped

¼ cup pickles, chopped

¼ cup green pepper, chopped

⅔ cup mayonnaise

1 tablespoon vinegar

1 teaspoon salt-free seasoning

1 tablespoon mustard

¼ cup onions, chopped

½ teaspoon salt

⅛ teaspoon pepper

INSTRUCTIONS

Gently mix together all ingredients until well blended. Chill.

Garnish with paprika, olives or tomatoes.

ADDITIONAL NOTES

The great thing about this basic recipe is that you can personalize it by adding other ingredients.

Other ideas to mix in: capers, green or black olives, any fresh, crunchy garden vegetables, like chopped kohlrabi.

Make the salad lower in fat, but still delicious, by substituting Greek yogurt for all or part of the mayonnaise.

PEOPLE SERVED: 8

MAIN DISHES

When I was growing up my mom had a vast collection of recipes that she kept in a disorganized pile in her pantry.

There were recipes clipped out of the newspaper in long, narrow strips, pages torn from magazines, and little cookbooks she picked up at the grocery store.

Sometimes when she wanted a particular recipe, she'd have to go through the whole pile to find it! Or she might sift through the pile for inspiration for that night's dinner. This **recipe** always seemed to make its way to the top of the pile!

KALEEN LONG

YORKSHIRE CRUST PIZZA

INGREDIENTS

1 cup milk

2 eggs

1 cup flour

½ teaspoon salt

Sauce, cheese, and pizza toppings of your choice.

INSTRUCTIONS

Heat oven to 400°F.

Place butter in a 13x9-inch dish and melt in oven while oven is coming to temperature. Remove from oven and tilt pan to coat with butter.

Pour crust batter in pan and bake 15 minutes. Reduce oven to 350°F. and bake 10 minutes more.

Remove from oven and top with your favorite sauce, cheese, and toppings. Return to oven for 5-10 minutes to melt cheese and warm toppings.

Don't be surprised - this buttery crust puffs unevenly in the oven.

PEOPLE SERVED: 4

MAIN DISHES

In the Philippines, the custom and traditions show a great deal of influence from the Spaniards who brought Christianity to the country.

To enjoy your visit to the islands, submerge yourself in the Filipino heritage. A great way to do this, is by enjoying each region's preparation, cooking and presentation of their respective ethnic cuisine.

My mother Dorie's Chicken Afritada dish is always a favorite, especially instead of eating lunch in the house. She serves it outside on a table lined with banana leaves, under the shades of the Acacia, Kayomito and Palm trees that surround our house.

Ice cold coconut water, lemonade and freshly picked tropical fruits are always available to indulge on for friends and family who happen to stop by to enjoy the day with us.

Those were the good old days!

ALITHA EDWARDS

DORIE'S CHICKEN AFRITADA

INGREDIENTS

2 to 3 pounds chicken, cut into serving pieces

2 cloves garlic, crushed

1 medium size onion, chopped

1 - 6 ounce can tomato sauce

1 bay leaf

1 tablespoon peppercorns

2 teaspoons salt

1 teaspoon ground black pepper

2 medium sized potatoes, cubed

¼ cup water

1 cup mushrooms

1 green bell pepper, sliced into strips

1 red bell pepper, sliced into strips

1 tablespoon sweet red bell pepper flakes

INSTRUCTIONS

Simmer chicken for about 15 to 20 minutes in garlic, onion, tomato sauce, bay leaf, peppercorns, salt, ground black pepper and water.

Add cubed potatoes and continue to cook until potatoes are tender.

Add mushrooms, green and red bell peppers.

Before turning off stove, sprinkle sweet red pepper flakes over cooked dish for some medium heat presentation.

Serve with steamed white rice.

PEOPLE SERVED: 4-6

MAIN DISHES

When we lived in Ellensburg, we would have a **BBQ every Labor Day weekend in conjunction with the Rodeo.**

We lived near the arena, and a lot of people would stop by. The party got so big over the years that even with two BBQs going, it was hard to keep up and my husband was spending all of his time at the grill.

So we decided to try adding pulled pork, which we made ahead and serving it in a crock pot. **People loved it and chose that over the burgers and hot dogs.**

We adjusted the recipe over the years and made more and more batches. It was great and

my husband got to relax and visit more the day of the BBQ.

WENDY RITTEREISER

PULLED PORK SLIDERS

INGREDIENTS

5 pounds pork (butt, or substitute shoulder)

⅓ cup yellow mustard

3 teaspoons liquid smoke

Rub

3 tablespoons paprika

2 tablespoons black pepper

2 teaspoons sugar

2 teaspoons salt

2 teaspoons cayenne pepper

Sauce

Pan drippings

1-2 cups ketchup

⅓ cup light molasses

2 tablespoons Worcestershire sauce

Salt, pepper and hot sauce to taste

PEOPLE SERVED: ABOUT 8

INSTRUCTIONS

Heat oven to 325°F.

Mix mustard with liquid smoke in a bowl and combine all dry ingredients in another bowl.

Cut or separate pork along fat lines so that you have thinner pieces with more surface area, rather than one large piece, and pat dry. Rub mustard mix over all sides of pork then sprinkle all sides with the dry mixture.

Place on rack over a baking sheet. Cover first with parchment paper then cover with foil and seal edges. (Parchment paper keeps the foil from touching and reacting with the mustard).

After about 4 hours remove foil and parchment to allow pork to brown and continue to cook until it reaches 200°F.

While pork cools, make BBQ sauce by pouring all pan drippings into fat separator and drain off as much fat as possible.

Add ketchup, molasses, Worcestershire and seasonings to taste. Shred pork and add sauce.

You can refrigerate and reheat in a crock pot when ready to serve.

Optional: If you have extra time and want even juicier pork, brine it in the refrigerator for a couple of hours before cooking in 4 quarts of water, 1 cup of salt, ½ cup sugar and 3 tablespoons liquid smoke.

MAIN DISHES

QUICK CHICKEN PIE

INGREDIENTS

2 9-inch, deep dish frozen pie shells

1 can mixed vegetables, drained

1 can cream of mushroom soup

1 small can chicken or cut up roasted chicken or turkey

1 tablespoon instant onion

1 cup shredded cheese

INSTRUCTIONS

Mix all vegetables, soup, chicken, onion and cheese. Pour into the bottom of a frozen pie shell.

Top with the other pie shell.

Cut slits in the shell for steam.

Bake at 400°F. for 40 minutes.

PEOPLE SERVED: 4

This is one recipe that our kids have always liked.

When our oldest daughter, who now lives in Missouri, calls and finds out we are having this for dinner, **she gets jealous!**

MARK MAXWELL

MAIN DISHES

This recipe was born out of necessity.

The night before the annual Harvest Potluck at work, as in 11 PM, I looked in the pantry. Pasta, always available in my home, cheese, ditto on availability, and Panko.

Who would think that the best bread crumbs in the world would come from Japan? **That is how this tasty spicy Mac & Cheese was inspired.**

It is dinner with a salad, or an amazing side dish with roasted chicken. For a special party dish, use this to make stuffed tomatoes. I hope you enjoy it! Oh yes, one more thing. **I actually am highly competitive at potlucks.** If my dish is *not* gone, I mean *scraped to the bottom,* it is considered a failure.

This was NOT a failure!

MALIA HASEGAWA

WHOA MAMA MAC & CHEESE

INGREDIENTS

1 ½ cups fusilli or elbow pasta

4 tablespoons butter, divided

¼ cup all-purpose flour

3 cups whole milk

1 teaspoon dry mustard

¾ teaspoon salt

½ teaspoon ground white pepper

1 tablespoon hot pepper sauce

1 cup shredded pepper jack cheese

1 ½ cups shredded sharp cheddar cheese

½ cup grated parmesan cheese

⅓ cup panko bread crumbs

2 teaspoons chili powder

PEOPLE SERVED: 6-8

INSTRUCTIONS

Preheat oven to 375°F.

Bring a large pot of lightly salted water to a boil. Add pasta and cook for 8 to 10 minutes or until al dente; drain.

In a large saucepan over medium heat, melt 2 tablespoons butter. Whisk in flour and cook, stirring 1 minute. A little at a time, whisk in milk, mustard, salt, pepper and hot sauce.

Bring to a gentle boil, stirring constantly. Boil 1 minute, then remove from heat and whisk in pepper jack, cheddar and parmesan until smooth.

Stir in cooked pasta and pour into shallow 2 quart baking dish.

Melt remaining 2 tablespoons butter. Stir in panko bread crumbs and chili powder. Sprinkle over macaroni mixture.

Bake for 27- 32 minutes.

Let stand 10 minutes before serving.

MAIN DISHES

This is a recipe that I created myself, which in itself is not much of a story. It did take many trials and errors before I got the recipe right. Later, I added the Wheat Germ as a way to get extra vitamins in without anyone knowing and it gave the recipe just a little extra crunch.

The real story came later. One day at school my son had an assignment to write a descriptive paragraph about one of his favorite foods. I did not know about the assignment until it had been completed and returned to him. I happened to be going through his school work and found it. **He had gone into detail about his mom's awesome chicken strips that she uses to make chicken wraps with.**

He used some very descriptive words to describe how it tasted and how much he liked them, but the one that really stuck out to me was the word **"Heavenly".**

He used the word *heavenly* to describe my chicken strips!

I had no idea he liked them so much. Now, whenever I make them, I can only hope they are still heavenly.

SHERI JOHNSON

HEAVENLY CHICKEN STRIPS

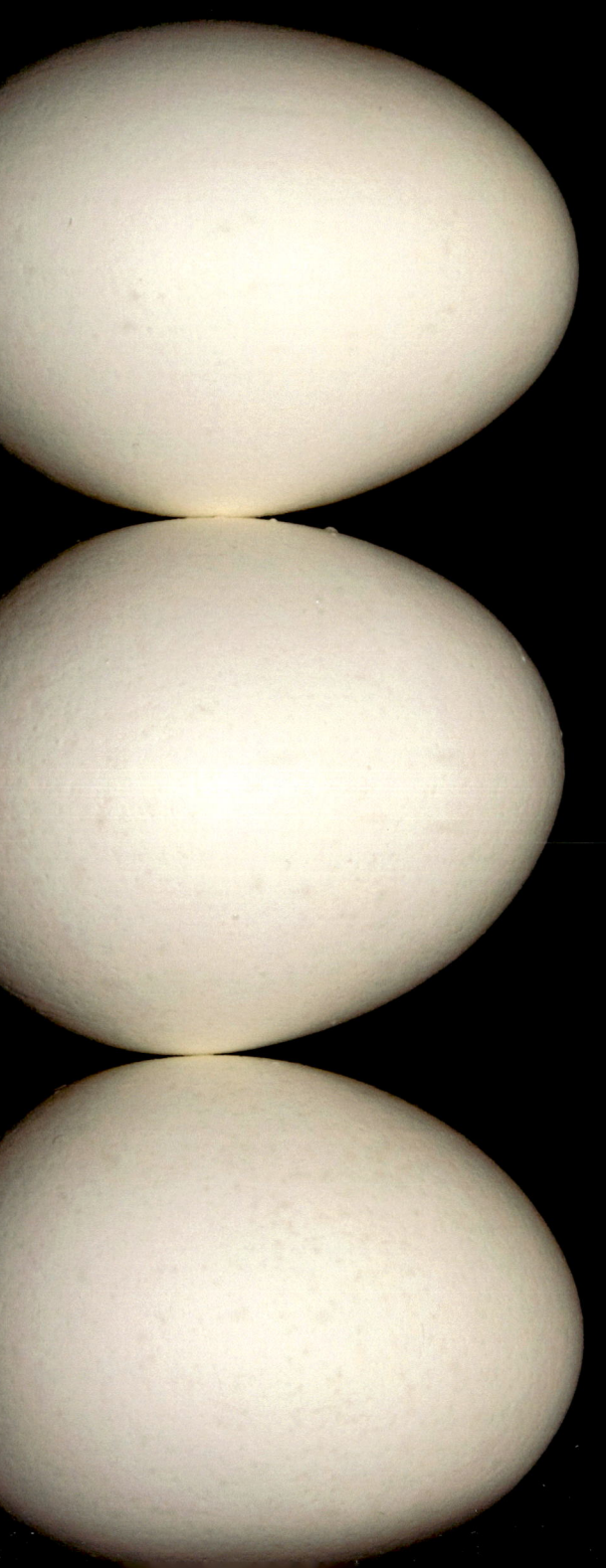

INGREDIENTS

3 boneless/skinless chicken breasts

3 eggs

4 tablespoons milk

¼ cup flour

1 ½ cups Italian bread crumbs

1 tablespoon wheat germ

1 teaspoon garlic salt

2 teaspoons Johnny's seasoning salt

2 tablespoons Italian seasoning

1 teaspoon oregano

2-3 tablespoons olive oil

INSTRUCTIONS

Mix eggs and milk in a medium to large bowl.

Slice chicken breasts into strips and place in egg mixture, set aside.

Mix flour, bread crumbs, and all seasonings in a large zip lock bag or a bowl with a lid.

Add 2 tablespoons of olive oil to large frying pan and heat.

Place 5 to 6 pieces of egg soaked chicken in the bread crumb mixture and coat completely. Place coated strips in frying pan. Repeat until all chicken is coated and in pan. Cook for 2-3 minutes or until golden brown, turn and cook the other side until golden brown. Remove from pan and place on paper towels.

These are great used in chicken wraps or dipped in ranch dressing or your favorite dipping sauce.

PEOPLE SERVED: 4 - 5

MAIN DISHES

This is one of my favorite dishes that Amy makes for me.

I have always enjoyed enchiladas and hers are my favorite.

KELLY FRAKES

CHICKEN AND CHEESE ENCHILADAS

INGREDIENTS

1 can - 10 ¾ ounces cream of chicken soup

½ cup sour cream

1 cup pace picante sauce

2 teaspoons chili powder

2 cups cooked chicken, chopped

½ cup shredded Monterey jack cheese

6 flour tortillas (6" long), warmed

1 small tomato, chopped

1 green onion, chopped

INSTRUCTIONS

Mix first four ingredients. Stir 1 cup of mixture with chicken and cheese.

Make enchiladas and place in 11x7½x2-inch pan.

Pour on remaining mixture.

Bake at 350°F. for 40 minutes.

PEOPLE SERVED: 6

MAIN DISHES

My husband, Stu, is originally from Vancouver, BC. and he still returns every year to fish off the **West Coast of Vancouver Island to a remote fishing lodge** that's **only accessible by boat.**

He brings home **80 - 100 pounds of Salmon and Halibut,** so we have a lot of fish recipes!

This is one of our **favorites for entertaining.** It's easy and almost tastes like candy.

DANA SIMPSON

CEDAR PLANK GRILLED SALMON

INGREDIENTS

4 pounds fresh sockeye salmon

2 - 6" x 12" cedar grilling plank

Marinade:

¾ cup dark soy sauce

1 ½ cups real maple syrup

2 tablespoons chopped fresh ginger

2 tablespoons chopped garlic

INSTRUCTIONS

Combine all marinade ingredients and blend well.

Cut the salmon into steaks and remove the skin. Pour marinade over salmon. Cover and refrigerate 2-4 hours.

Soak cedar plank in warm water for at least 20 minutes.

Pre-heat grill, then turn down to medium-high heat. Place drained cedar planks in center of grill. Place salmon directly on cedar plank and grill 12-15 minutes.

Remove salmon from planks and finish directly on the BBQ grate, 2-3 minutes.

PEOPLE SERVED: 12

MAIN DISHES

Coconut has found a special place in many hearts these days!

If you are one of those people who can't get enough of coconut, coconut water, coconut flakes... here is a new one for you - *Coconut Rice.*

This coconut rice has a robust flavor and texture and changes your blank canvas of rice to a dish that will steal the show!

LAVANYA VENKATESWAR

COCONUT RICE

INGREDIENTS

2 cups basmati or long grain rice

1 large onion, sliced

1 large carrot, diced

¼ cup green peas

1 cup fresh grated coconut or unsweetened dried coconut

½ cup coconut milk

1 tablespoon butter

3 cloves

1 inch long cinnamon stick

2 green cardamoms

2 bay leaves

1 ½ teaspoons salt

For garnishing:

2 tablespoons cashew nuts, sautéed in butter

INSTRUCTIONS

Heat butter in a pan until melted and add the cloves, cinnamon stick, bay leaves, cardamom seeds and sliced onions. Sauté until the onions are golden brown.

Add the carrots and peas and sauté for another 2 minutes.

Add the rice, coconut milk, fresh grated coconut, salt and 4 cups water. Cook on low flame until the rice is cooked.

Garnish with cashew nuts sautéed in butter and serve hot!

ADDITIONAL NOTES

Frozen grated coconut is available at any Asian store and can be used as a substitute for fresh grated coconut.

PEOPLE SERVED: 4

MAIN DISHES

Every Filipino has his own version of the "Pork Barbecue" as we fondly call it. My version, of course, is a family favorite.

Summers meant baseball games at the cul de sac, popsicles from the ice cream man, splashing in the inflatable pool and daddy's barbecue for dinner. **To this day, it's still on my kids' request list when they come home for a visit.** Our neighbors knew what was for dinner on most summer nights. Many years ago I had a garage sale and I thought I would lure more shoppers in if I sold my Pork Barbecue on the side.

To make a long story short, **I made more money from the Barbecue than from the garage sale.**

NANCY DACQUEL

BARBECUE ON A STICK

INGREDIENTS

2 pounds meat (pork loin or chicken thigh), sliced approximately 2"x 2" x 0.25"

½ cup light soy sauce

1 lemon

½ cup banana ketchup

2 teaspoons salt

1 teaspoon ground black pepper

2 tablespoons brown sugar

8-10 cloves garlic, minced

Bamboo skewers

PEOPLE SERVED: 6-8

INSTRUCTIONS

Combine meat, soy sauce, lemon juice, ketchup, salt, ground black pepper, brown sugar, and chopped garlic in a mixing bowl. Mix the ingredients well. Mixing by hand is recommended, making sure all meat slices are evenly coated.

Marinate the meat for at least 3 hours or overnight, allowing the meat to absorb all the flavors.

Soak the bamboo skewers for 30 minutes or longer. This will prevent the skewers from burning on the grill. Take a bamboo skewer and thread at least 5 to 6 slices of meat per stick. Threading them more compactly (but not too much) will prevent the meat from drying out.

Add a few tablespoons of soy sauce, ketchup, and a tablespoon of cooking oil to the leftover marinade to create the basting sauce. Grill the meat on medium heat until both sides are done. Start basting only after the meat is thoroughly cooked but not over-grilled. If you baste too early, the sauce will burn before the meat is cooked.

Enjoy the Barbecue as an appetizer or as a main dish with a steaming bowl of rice and a salad on the side.

ADDITIONAL NOTES

Banana ketchup is slightly sweeter than regular tomato ketchup and is available at any Asian store. You may substitute it with regular ketchup if you prefer. A quick basting sauce can also be made by mixing any bottled honey barbecue sauce with orange juice and a dash of hot sauce (optional).

MAIN DISHES

This is my dad's recipe.

Growing up in the coast of Perú, our family spent long days at the beach during summer. **At sunset, local fishermen would offer what they fished and my dad would buy the whole basket of fresh fish.**

At home, my dad would make this ever light and simple recipe, but *always so full of flavor* for mom and us.

I now make this recipe often and share my childhood memories with my children and husband.

ZORY QUINDE-AXTELL

SUDADO DE PESCADO *(BRAISED FISH IN SPICY ONION AND TOMATO SAUCE)*

INGREDIENTS

6 whole fresh fish cleaned, scaled and gutted, (fillets work as well)

½ cup Andean beer (chicha, fermented corn beverage)

2 tablespoons vegetable oil

2 cloves garlic, crushed

½ teaspoon annatto powder

2 medium red onions, sliced

2 yellow chili peppers (ajíes Amarillo), seeded and sliced

1 red bell pepper, peeled and sliced

3 tomatoes, sliced

1 tablespoon freshly chopped cilantro

Salt and freshly ground pepper

To serve: 2 large white potatoes, cut into oval spheres and steamed.

INSTRUCTIONS

Season fish with salt and pepper.

Heat oil in a large skillet and sauté garlic over medium heat until golden, about 2 minutes. Add annatto powder and yellow chili peppers; sauté for 2 minutes.

Place one layer of fish on the skillet; add a layer of onions and then a layer of tomatoes. Then add Andean beer and bring to a boil.

Lower the heat, add cilantro and cover and simmer fish for 6 or 8 minutes until fish is just turning opaque and is almost ready. Be careful not to overcook.

Serve fish in a deep dish. Accompany with steamed potatoes.

PEOPLE SERVED: 6

With **8 kids to feed** my grandparents, Ken & Kay Maher (mom's side), had to be thrifty. But according to my grandfather, budget had nothing to do with the high frequency of pigs feet being served at the Maher house.

The man simply loved his pigs feet and whenever we visited their house in Mossy Rock, WA, we were treated to this swiney delicacy. Without fail, he would remind us that the foot is the most underrated part of a pig.

You know you're loved when you serve pigs feet and people still visit.

My grandfather passed away a couple of years ago. I haven't had pigs feet since, but submitting this recipe reminds me that it's high time my kids experience the most underrated part of a pig.

ANDY HEILY

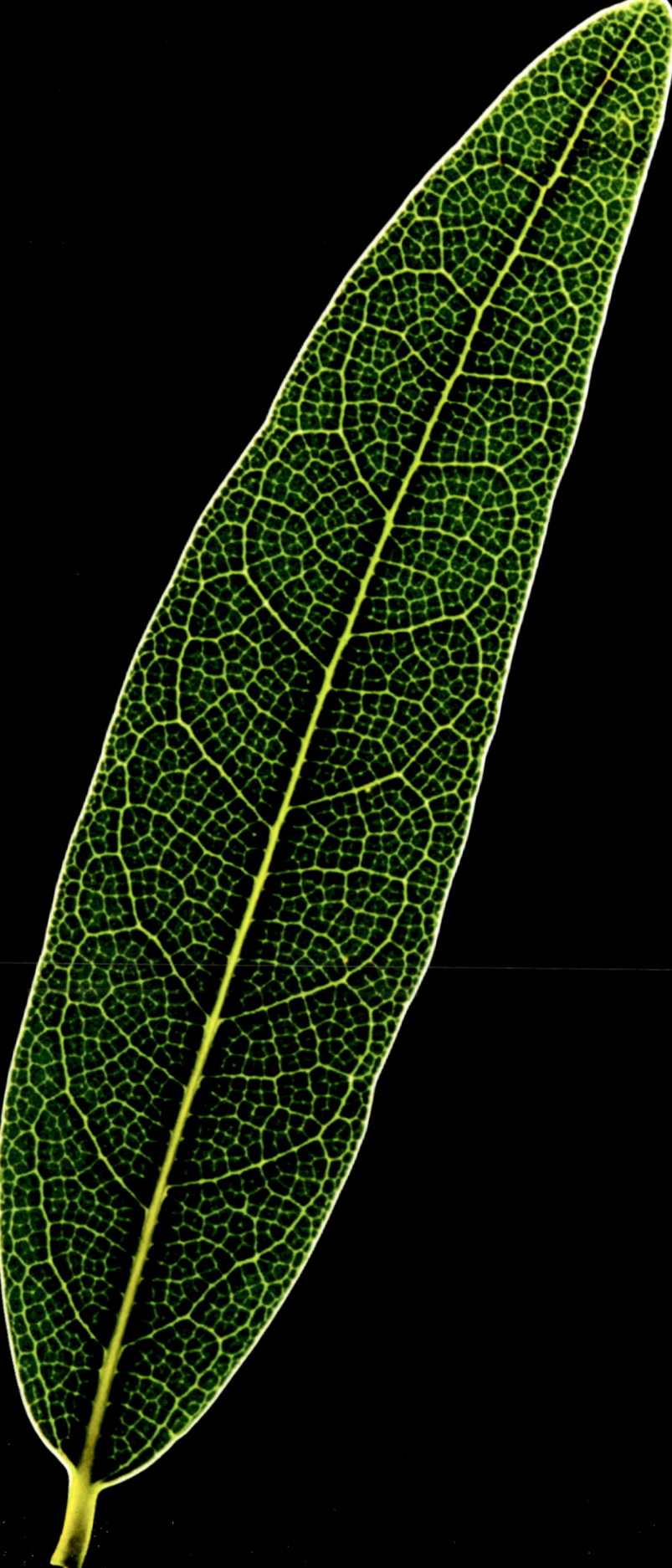

GRANDPA MAHER'S PIGS FEET

INGREDIENTS

8 pigs' feet

1 onion, diced

¾ cup vinegar

2 tablespoons garlic, chopped

1 teaspoon pepper

2 tablespoons seasoning salt

4 bay leaves

Enough water to cover & boil feet

INSTRUCTIONS

Wash pigs' feet in cold water and place into a large pot or Dutch oven.

Add onion, vinegar, seasoned salt, garlic, black pepper, and bay leaves to the feet; pour in water to cover. Bring to a boil, reduce heat to low, and simmer until meat is tender and falling off the bones, about 2 hours.

PEOPLE SERVED: 4

MAIN DISHES

This recipe was created by my wife and me,

as we wanted to create a flavorful pasta dish using whole grain pasta and lean meat.

This recipe was an instant hit!

JORDAN SMITH

PENNE PASTA WITH SMOKED SAUSAGE AND ROASTED TOMATOES

INGREDIENTS

10 ounces 100% whole wheat penne pasta

14-16 ounces smoked turkey sausage links, cut into half-moons on the bias

10 ounces cherry tomatoes, cut in half

1 medium onion, halved and sliced thin

4 ounces shredded parmesan cheese

4 ounces pasta sauce

1 ounce fresh basil, finely sliced

2 tablespoons olive oil

3 cloves garlic, finely diced

½ teaspoon red pepper flakes

Salt and pepper to taste

INSTRUCTIONS

Preheat oven to 350°F.

Toss halved tomatoes with 1 tablespoon of olive oil, salt and pepper to taste.

Spray cookie sheet with cooking spray or lightly grease with oil and arrange tomatoes in a single layer. Bake for 20-25 minutes. Remove tomatoes from oven and set aside.

In a large pot, boil salted water for pasta. Cook pasta as directed on package.

Heat a large skillet to medium heat and add 1 tablespoon of olive oil. After oil is heated, add sausage. Sauté until browned. Add onion. Cook until onion begins to soften (1-2 minutes). Add garlic and red pepper flakes and cook for 1-2 minutes more. Add roasted tomatoes and pasta sauce. Mix well and heat 1-2 minutes.

Add cooked pasta and remove from heat. Toss with shredded parmesan cheese and finely sliced basil.

Enjoy!

PEOPLE SERVED: 3-4

My wife grew up in Chicago living in a two-story flat; her family on the bottom floor and her Italian grandmother above.

It goes without saying she spent a great deal of time in the kitchen with her grandma observing and helping with the cooking.

Although her grandma did not leave behind any written recipes, her many hours in the kitchen with her granddaughter taught her the basics and a love for Italian cooking.

These meatballs are a healthier version, with all the flavor of the meatballs she made with her grandma.

BRETT ALLISON

ITALIAN MEATBALLS
(WITH KRETSCHMER TOASTED WHEAT GERM)

INGREDIENTS

1 pound ground turkey (domestic or wild)

1 pound ground pork

1 pound ground beef (can substitute with deer or elk)

1 tablespoon kosher salt

1 teaspoon ground pepper

1 tablespoon dried basil

2 cloves garlic, finely chopped

½ cup grated Parmesan cheese

1 egg

½ cup Kretschmer toasted wheat germ

¼ cup Kretschmer toasted wheat bran

¼ cup WildRoots ground flax seed

INSTRUCTIONS

Heat oven to 300°F.

Combine all ingredients in a large bowl until all ingredients are mixed well.

Roll meat into 1 ½ inch meat balls.

Place in pan(s) about 1 to 2 inches apart.

Pour red wine (your choice of wine) over meatballs, just enough to cover the bottom of the pan.

Cover pan(s) with tin foil.

Place in oven for 30-40 minutes

Serve with your favorite red sauce – add the juice and bits of flavor in the bottom of the pan to your sauce to add another layer of flavor.

PEOPLE SERVED: 6-8

MAIN DISHES

This recipe has been a family favorite for many years. **Usually, it is the first item gone when our family has a reunion or potluck.**

When I worked 3rd shift, our shift was always having a potluck and not for any particular reason. At one of these potlucks, I brought in meatloaf and several people asked who made it.

Mark Powell was telling everyone he had made it and they were complimenting him on how great it was.

Someone happened to come into the lab telling everyone that Mark had made the best meatloaf. **I said thank you for saying so.** They were bewildered why I thanked them. Mark had everyone believing he had made the meatloaf. **I named this recipe Mark's Meatloaf.**

MARK'S MEATLOAF

INGREDIENTS

3 pounds ground chuck

1 small onion, chopped

1 green pepper, chopped

3 large eggs

1 - 6 ounce can tomato paste

1 - 5.5 ounce can 100% vegetable juice, regular or spicy

¼ cup Worcestershire sauce

½ cup ketchup

1 sleeve saltine crackers, crushed

2 cups quick oats

1 cup dried bread crumbs

Topping:

1 ½ cups ketchup

¼ cup Worcestershire sauce

INSTRUCTIONS

Hand mix all ingredients.

Form into loaf using 13X9-inch glass or foil pan.

Spread topping on uncooked meatloaf.

Bake at 350°F. for 1 hour.

The secret to the meatloaf is the 100% vegetable juice.

PEOPLE SERVED: 8-10

MAIN DISHES

My fondness for cooking began of course with watching my mother (her specialty: Tuna Casserole with Potato Chips, timeless), but I was also influenced by my **Russian grandmother.** She spoke English, but had that cool Russian accent. She left Russia in 1918 prior to the communist takeover, moved to Shanghai, survived with my mom through concentration camps and Japanese occupation, only to leave on the last boat to San Francisco before the Chinese Communists took over. **Food and cooking were a big part of my interaction with her.**

Imagine a 5'2" babushka cooking for 5 boys!

She would work all day and night, and give us each a paper bag filled with piroshky for school lunch the next day. **She probably made a 100 at a time, and they were gone in an instant because they were fabulous!**

KARL VAN VLEET

PIROSHKY

INGREDIENTS

Piroshky:

Sour-cream pastry *(see below)*

2 tablespoons butter

3 cups finely chopped onions

1 pound ground beef

Salt, if desired

Freshly ground pepper

3 hard-cooked eggs, finely chopped, about one cup

¼ cup finely chopped dill

1 egg, lightly beaten

3 tablespoons water

Sour-cream pastry:

3 ½ cups flour

Salt, if desired

1 teaspoon baking powder

½ cup butter, chilled and cut into small pieces

2 eggs

1 cup sour cream

PEOPLE SERVED:
YIELD 30 PIROSHKY

INSTRUCTIONS

Sour-cream pastry preparation:

Put 3 ¼ cups of the flour, salt to taste, baking powder, butter, eggs and sour cream into the container of a food processor. Process until thoroughly blended.

If a food processor is not used, put the flour, salt to taste and baking powder in a mixing bowl. Add the butter and cut it with two knives or a pastry blender until the mixture looks like coarse cornmeal. Using a fork, add the eggs and thoroughly blend.

Scrape the mixture out onto a lightly floured board and knead as briefly as possible, using as little flour as possible to make smooth and workable dough.

Shape the dough into a flat cake and wrap it in plastic wrap. Chill until ready to use. YIELD Two pounds of dough

Piroshky preparation:

Prepare the pastry and chill it. Preheat oven to 400°F.

Heat the butter in a skillet and add the onions. Cook, stirring, until the onions are wilted.

Add the beef and, using a heavy metal kitchen spoon, stir and chop down to break up any lumps in the meat. Cook until meat loses its raw look. Add salt and pepper to taste.

Add the chopped egg and dill. Stir to blend. There should be about four cups. Remove to a mixing bowl and let cool.

Roll out the pastry as thinly as possible (less than one-eighth inch thick). Using a 3 ½ -5-inch cookie cutter, cut the dough into rounds. We used a 4 inch cookie cutter to produce 30 rounds. The dough will shrink after cutting. You may roll out the circles or rounds to make them larger or you may stretch them carefully by hand. Beat the egg with the water. Brush the top of each pastry round with the egg mixture.

Use about two tablespoons of filling for each circle of dough. Shape the filling into an oval and place it on half of the circle of dough. Fold the other half of the circle of dough over to enclose the filling. Press the edges of the dough with the fingers or the tines of a fork to seal. Brush the tops with egg mixture to seal.

Arrange the filled pieces on a lightly greased baking sheet.

Place in the oven and bake 25 minutes.

MAIN DISHES

My grandma originated from the Midwest.

She was a wonderful cook and like many farm-women, **she didn't have a cookbook or recipes that were written down.**

They were passed down from the women in her family and resided in her head. Midwest Salisbury Steak is a **Sunday family supper recipe.**

All the daughters and daughters-in-law were required to participate in dinner prep and that is how

they learned the family recipes.

After dinner they were asked to rid-up the table *(which meant to gather up the dirty dishes).*

SHELLEY VANDERPOEL

GRANDMA PUDERBAUGH'S
MIDWEST SALISBURY STEAK

INGREDIENTS

Steak Patties:

1 ½ pounds hamburger

1 medium sweet onion, chopped

½ sleeve saltine crackers, crushed

1 egg, whisked

½ teaspoon pepper

1 teaspoon salt

½ cup tomato juice

1 cup flour

Sauce (gravy):

32 ounces tomato juice

¾ cup white sugar

2 tablespoons chili powder

INSTRUCTIONS

Steak Patties:

Mix all together and form into hamburger style patties. Coat both sides of patties with flour (about 1 cup in a flat dish).

Heat ¼ cup vegetable oil in a large frying pan. When heated, put patties in pan and brown on each side for 2-3 minutes. Remove from pan and add sauce (gravy).

Cook for about 5 minutes and then return patties to pan. Simmer patties in tomato juice for about 20-30 minutes. Sauce should be kind of thick, almost like ketchup.

PEOPLE SERVED: 6

MAIN DISHES

This is a recipe that my wife and I have been refining for years.

We not only cook the ribs throughout the year, but they have become a regular item on my deer camp menu. **For the last 25 years,** a group of close friends have met up at my farm for the opening of the Missouri deer season, which has evolved into an all-inclusive hunt that entails a gourmet dinner each night.

One of the highlights of the hunt has always been the Rib dinner.

BRETT ALLISON

SMOKED BABY BACK RIBS

INGREDIENTS

3 slabs baby back ribs

Cider vinegar

2 tablespoons brown sugar

8 teaspoons kosher salt

2 teaspoons ancho chipotle pepper

2 teaspoons ground coriander

2 teaspoons dried oregano

2 teaspoons onion powder

2 teaspoons garlic powder

2 teaspoons smoked paprika

INSTRUCTIONS

Rib preparation:

Pull the fine layer of skin off the back of the ribs.

Mix all the dry ingredients in a bowl.

Brush both sides of the ribs with the cider vinegar.

Rub the seasoning on both sides of the ribs.

Cover and place in the refrigerator for 18 to 24 hours.

Cooking:

On either a wood fired smoker or a pellet smoker, bring the temperature up to 225°F.

Place the ribs on the rack, meaty side up.

Cook for 3 to 4 hours - you can spray with a liquid of your choice (beer, apple juice, water) every half hour but it's not necessary.

For "dry" ribs, there is nothing more to do but wait.

For "sticky or wet" ribs, coat the ribs with your favorite BBQ sauce 1 hour prior and then again 30 minutes before removing from the grill.

PEOPLE SERVED: 7- 9

The old adage that **"friends are the family you choose"** is certainly true in my life. I met my girlfriends Barbie and Cindi in the mid 80's in the basic Mountaineers climbing course, literally on top of a mountain, with no idea that they would become the people that I would celebrate birthdays and holidays with for the next several decades. Many years ago, Barbie invited us over for dinner. I asked what she was making and she replied that she found a new recipe she wanted to try and wasn't sure how it was going to turn out, **so we were going to be her lab rats for this experimental dish.**

I don't even remember what the dinner was, but the phrase **"Lab Rats for Dinner"** was immediately accepted into our lexicon and meant it's a surprise, no guarantees how good it will be, but it will be fun and interesting.

One day I stumbled across an intriguing recipe and it was Lab Rat time. Everything went fine until the final stage, which was to reduce the port wine sauce. I was drinking wine and visiting and when I returned to the kitchen, it wasn't just thick, it was a tarry sludge.

After muttering a few swear words, Cindi came to my rescue, reconstituting the sauce to a liquid consistency with some additional port. **It was delish!**

Of all the things I have cooked over the years, this is my most requested dinner.

SUE ENGDAHL-SHAVER

CHICKEN WITH PEARS AND PORT,
AN EPIC LAB RAT DINNER!

INGREDIENTS

3 firm ripe fresh pears, peeled, cored and cut into ½" chunks

3 teaspoons ground coriander

2 teaspoons ground cardamom

1 teaspoon black pepper

½ teaspoons cayenne pepper

1 tablespoon salt

3 tablespoons olive oil

12 boneless, skinless chicken thighs, organic

2 shallots, thinly sliced

6 cloves fresh garlic, sliced

1 unpeeled lemon, sliced

1 cup port wine, plus extra as needed

¼ cup fresh flat leaf parsley for garnishing

INSTRUCTIONS

Preheat oven to 375°F.

In a small bowl, mix the spices and salt and sprinkle each piece of chicken liberally on both sides with the spice mixture.

In a large nonstick skillet, heat the oil of medium high temperature until hot. Sauté the chicken until it is a golden brown. As the pieces are browned, place them in a 10x15-inch baking pan.

Sauté the pears, shallots, garlic and lemon for about 1 minute. Add the port and stir to scrape up the browned bits on the bottom of the pan. Bring just to a boil and then add the hot mixture with all of the goodies to the roasting pan, pouring it around (not over) the chicken to keep the browned crust intact.

Roast for about 40 to 45 minutes, or until the chicken reaches an internal temperature of 165°F. (Chicken will gain another 5°F. on standing).

Transfer the chicken to a platter and cover to keep warm. Using a slotted spoon, retrieve the pears, shallots, garlic and lemon slices and distribute them around the edges of the chicken so the skin stays nice and crisp.

Place the roasting pan on a burner on medium-high heat and cook to reduce the sauce to about ¾ cup. Adjust seasoning to taste and drizzle the sauce over the chicken and the goodies. This is the stage where I over-reduced the sauce and added more port in – I recommend this technique if you have the patience. Garnish with fresh parsley and serve with rice pilaf or whatever you fancy.

PEOPLE SERVED: 6

MAIN DISHES

Coming from a large family (6 children), mealtimes needed to be nourishing, filling, and easy; all while on a tight budget.

My family would make this dish during the cold winter months in Wisconsin when we needed to warm up after a fun day of sledding, skating or just playing in the snow.

We looked forward to this simple dish warming us up from the inside out. This is one of those go-to recipes that my family has when we want **good ol' comfort food.**

It always reminds me of back home in Wisconsin.

EMILY THOMPSON

DOWN HOME HEARTY GOULASH

INGREDIENTS

2 pounds lean ground beef

2 large yellow onions, chopped

3 cloves garlic, chopped

3 cups water

2 - 15 ounce cans tomato sauce

2 - 14.5 ounce cans diced tomatoes

3 tablespoons soy sauce

2 tablespoons dried Italian herb seasoning

3 bay leaves

1 tablespoon salt, to taste

2 cups uncooked elbow macaroni

PEOPLE SERVED: 8

INSTRUCTIONS

In large Dutch oven, cook and stir the ground beef over medium-high heat, breaking the meat up as it cooks until the meat is no longer pink and has started to brown (about 10 minutes).

Skim off excess fat and stir in the onions and garlic. Cook and stir the mixture until the onions are translucent (about 10 more minutes).

Stir in water, tomato sauce, diced tomatoes, soy sauce, Italian seasoning, bay leaves and salt and bring the mixture to a boil over medium heat. Reduce heat to low, cover and simmer 20 minutes, stirring occasionally.

Stir in the macaroni, cover and simmer over low heat until the pasta is tender (about 25 minutes), stirring occasionally.

Remove from heat, discard the bay leaves and enjoy!

MAIN DISHES

I loved Sundays. We'd get to go to a singing, joyful church service, and then my mama would come home and put on her special apron and make her **"special Sunday chicken dinner"**!

We would use her grama's delicate blue flowered china dishes (she never made us set the table on Sundays).

As she dropped each piece of chicken into the hot oil in the big iron skillet on the stove, she would always say to me:

"Christine, a good cook never leaves the stove while she is frying, don't forget that."

I remember the amazing smell! My tummy would growl like a bear. Even in summer, when my twin brother and I were outside playing in the sprinklers, that smell would draw me inside!

Mama always served Sunday's Special Fried Chicken on my great grama's blue flowered platter with perfectly mashed potatoes and sliced tomatoes. **It was the very best meal ever!**

MAMA'S SPECIAL SUNDAY FRIED CHICKEN

INGREDIENTS

1 whole fresh cut-up chicken

2 cups all-purpose flour

2 beaten eggs

¾ cup cold milk

2 tablespoons salt

2 tablespoons pepper

1 tablespoon ground mustard

1 tablespoon dried thyme

1 teaspoon fresh chopped garlic (or more if desired)

Oil for frying / thermometer

PEOPLE SERVED: 6

INSTRUCTIONS

Whisk dry ingredients and garlic in a medium baking dish.

Whisk milk and eggs in a medium bowl.

Pour oil into a 10x12-inch cast-iron skillet or other heavy straight-sided skillet (not nonstick) to a depth of ¾". Heat over medium-high heat until thermometer registers 350°F. Meanwhile, set a wire rack inside a large rimmed baking sheet.

Working with 1 chicken piece at a time (use 1 hand for wet ingredients and the other for dry ingredients), dip chicken in egg/milk mixture, allowing excess to drip back into bowl. Dredge in flour mixture; tap against bowl to shake off excess. Place 5 pieces of chicken in skillet.

Fry chicken, turning with tongs every 1–2 minutes and adjusting heat to maintain a steady temperature of 300°–325°F., until skin is deep golden brown and an instant-read thermometer inserted into thickest part of chicken registers 165°F., about 10 minutes for wings and 12 minutes for thighs, legs, and breasts.

Using tongs, remove chicken from skillet, allowing excess oil to drip back into skillet. Transfer chicken to prepared rack.

Repeat with remaining chicken pieces; let cool for at least 10 minutes before serving.

Enjoy!

CHRISSY KENADY-HARVEY

MAIN DISHES

When I was 15 years old, my mother had laid the chicken out for dumplings and asked me to fix this for our dinner. I had **helped my mother cook this meal many times.**

While adding the dumplings I stirred the pot, added more dumplings and stirred again. After adding all the dumplings and putting the chicken and evaporated milk in, I stirred it again. While the dumplings were finishing cooking, *I stirred and stirred and stirred.*

When my parents came home, my mother looked in the pot and started laughing. She asked me how much I stirred the dumplings and as I explained to her how I made the dumplings, my daddy came in and looked at the pot and immediately took it outside and threw it away. He told my mother that this was the most expensive meal the dogs had ever had. **My mother then explained to me that I had stirred my dumplings too much and had in fact just made a big pot of mush.**

I never tried to make dumplings again until I started working here at Continental Mills. We had a potluck dinner and I was asked if I could make chicken and dumplings. I made a pot and brought it to our dinner. **Everyone loved them** and wanted my recipe.

PAULA HANRAHAN

CHICKEN AND DUMPLINGS

INGREDIENTS

1 bag frozen boneless chicken tenders or chicken breasts

5-6 cubes chicken bouillon

1 - 5 ounce can Carnation evaporated milk

1 package frozen dumplings (found in freezer section at Walmart)

¼ teaspoon garlic pepper

1 large stew pot

PEOPLE SERVED: 8

INSTRUCTIONS

Thaw chicken then place in pot filling pot half full of water.

Put chicken bouillon in with chicken and cook until done or no longer pink inside. Remove chicken from broth and let cool.

Bring broth to a rolling boil. Take frozen dumplings and separate layers and break into three pieces each and drop a few at a time into boiling broth stirring occasionally.

Keep dropping dumplings a few at a time until all dumplings are used, stirring occasionally. Shred chicken and place back into pot with dumplings.

Add the evaporated milk and cook for about 25 minutes at low heat setting. Broth will thicken while cooking.

MAIN DISHES

We had just moved into our family home, where my mom still lives. There's a greenbelt behind the house that many neighbors had fenced in as an extension of their backyard. My mom and step-dad disagreed on how large our backyard was with the additional green space included.

Mom had her number, he had his and mom kept telling him he was *"full of beans"*.

Obviously she thought she was right. So Monday came and he went to work. **Mom promptly got her measuring tape and a kid as a helper to measure the entire fence line,** writing the measurements down as they went. When she was all finished and had the final number, low and behold...

she was WRONG! *He was right!*

But, she still wanted to have fun with it. **So she made this meal and printed up a HUGE banner to post across the garage door for him when he got home from work.**

It said "BEANS DEAR BEANS" and we had beans for dinner that night.

RACHYL MILLER

BEANS DEAR BEANS

INGREDIENTS

1 pound ground beef

1 pound bacon

1 onion

30 ounces (2 cans) pork 'n' beans

15 ounces (1 can) kidney beans, drained

15 ounces (1 can) garbanzo beans, drained

1 cup ketchup

¼ cup brown sugar

1 tablespoon liquid smoke

3 tablespoons vinegar

1 teaspoon salt

Pepper to taste

INSTRUCTIONS

Brown hamburger, chopping while browning. Set aside.

Cook bacon and onions together.

Put cooked hamburger, bacon and onions in crock pot.

Add remaining ingredients. Cook on high 4-6 hours, or low 6-8 hours.

PEOPLE SERVED: 8

MAIN DISHES

On our first date in college my wife made this traditional Indonesian rice dish for me...it was fantastic and I was hooked (on both the food and my wife)!

The back story on the recipe...

My Dutch mother-in-law grew up in Indonesia - a Dutch colony at the time - and mastered many delicious Indonesian recipes that we enjoy together at family gatherings.

We always make extra Nasi Goreng since it tastes even better the next day!

BOB WALLACH

NASI GORENG
INDONESIAN FRIED RICE

INGREDIENTS

1 ½ pounds pork tenderloin

3 large yellow onions

2 cups jasmine long grain white rice

3 tablespoons coconut oil

Spices:

- Soy sauce
- Brown sugar
- Coriander
- Sambal oelek
- Curry
- Salt
- Black pepper

ADDITIONAL NOTES

You can substitute ground beef for pork tenderloin if you like. You can also substitute brown rice for a healthier version.

Sambal Oelek can usually be found in the international section of the grocery store or on Amazon. Sambal Oelek is fairly spicy, so if you prefer a milder heat level, adjust accordingly.

Traditionally, Nasi Goreng is served with a fried egg on top, but we prefer to cut an omelet into strips. You can add sautéed green onions and tomatoes for more color.

PEOPLE SERVED: 8

INSTRUCTIONS

Onions - Chop the onions finely. Heat 1 tablespoon coconut oil in a large heavy frying pan over medium heat, add onions. Stir frequently. When the onions start to brown turn heat down to low. The goal is to cook the onions slowly until they are tender and brown (not crispy). This can take a half hour to an hour.

Rice – While onions are cooking heat ½ tablespoon coconut oil in large pot and add 2 cups of rice over low heat. Stir frequently until rice starts to turn golden brown (about 5 minutes). Add 3 ½ cups of water and ½ teaspoon of salt. Cover pot, heat to boiling, stir once, and then let simmer until water is absorbed and rice is done.

Pork – Cut 1 ½ pounds pork tenderloin into cubes (about the size of dice). Combine 2 teaspoons coriander, 1 teaspoon curry, ½ teaspoon black pepper, and ½ teaspoon salt in a small bowl. While the onions and rice are cooking, thoroughly mix the spices with the pork to flavor the pork.

Marinate the pork while onions and rice are cooking.

When the rice is almost done, it's time to cook the pork. Heat 1 tablespoon coconut oil in a large frying pan and add the pork. Stir frequently to insure browning on all sides (about 2 minutes should do).

Combining It All Together – In a small bowl mix 2 tablespoons soy sauce with 2 teaspoons brown sugar, 1 teaspoon coriander and 2 teaspoons sambal oelek. stir the spice mixture into the onions, but be sure the onion pan is not hot (otherwise soy sauce can get a burnt flavor). Then combine the spicy onion mixture with the meat and stir thoroughly. Finally, mix that all in with the rice and you're ready to eat!

MAIN DISHES

My family loves this roast, especially on cold days.

The beer adds a great flavor!!!

CINDY LAMAR

BEER PORK ROAST

INGREDIENTS

Choose a good size pork roast, type is your choice but make sure it is not too big and can fit in the bottom of a large, deep pot.

1 bottle dark beer, your choice of brand

3 cloves garlic

3 stalks celery

3 carrots

Potatoes
(enough to fill the bottom of your roasting pan)

Any other vegetables of your choice

1 can of beef broth

3 tablespoons oil

Salt, pepper and any other seasonings you like

INSTRUCTIONS

Preheat oven to 325°F.

Cut up your vegetables, except potatoes, and set aside.

In a large deep pot, on medium heat, place the oil and let warm up. Rub your seasonings on your roast.

Place the roast and the garlic in the pot – you are going to simmer the roast on each side for approximately 5 minutes.

Place the meat in your roaster pan. Scrape the bottom of your roasting pan and add your beer, broth, vegetables, except potatoes, and let simmer for approximately 10 minutes until vegetables are just starting to become soft.

Pour over your roast in the roaster pan.

Cut your potatoes up, skin on or off, and add to roaster pan. Cover with aluminum foil and place pan in preheated oven.

Cook on 325°F. for approximately 1 to 1 ½ hours – depends on how you like your meat to be cooked *(can remove foil and let skin crisp up - can even cook last 5 minutes or so under broiler).*

Take out and serve!

PEOPLE SERVED: 6 - 8

MAIN DISHES

The kids always ask if we're having the Turkey Tetrazzini dish when they come home for *Thanksgiving weekend.*

It is a **tradition** with our family and we look forward to sharing it each year while we **gather around the table** sharing our family news.

This dish is great for serving the day after Thanksgiving when you have all the leftovers from the big dinner and are looking for a new and creative way to combine them into one dish.

HEATHER DAVIS

TURKEY TETRAZZINI

INGREDIENTS

8 ounce can or ½ pound mushrooms, sliced

½ pound noodles (wide or spaghetti)

6 tablespoons butter

2 tablespoons flour

2 cups hot turkey or chicken broth

1 cup whipping cream, unwhipped

3 tablespoons sherry (or cooking sherry)

¼ teaspoon nutmeg

2 cups chopped, cooked turkey

¼ cup grated parmesan cheese

INSTRUCTIONS

Cook noodles in boiling water until tender. Sauté mushrooms and butter over low heat.

Prepare Sauce in this order:

Melt 3 tablespoons butter.

Stir in flour, broth, then whipping cream, unwhipped. Cook sauce over low heat 8 minutes, stirring frequently.

Add sherry and nutmeg to sauce, stir. Salt & pepper to taste.

Combine:

In large, buttered baking casserole dish combine noodles, sauce and buttered mushrooms.

Add chopped turkey, stir and spread in dish. Sprinkle top with grated parmesan cheese.

Bake at 350°F. for 20+ minutes.

PEOPLE SERVED: FAMILY SIZE - 6

MAIN DISHES

We started our annual trip to Panama City Beach FL in the early 90s. During one of those trips we came across a little Italian Bistro that had **the best Lasagna** that we had ever had.

We continue to frequent the Italian Bistro and it became our Anniversary dinner spot. We had many family members that went on the trips and some time it was just me and Susie, but we always made it back to that restaurant.

Susie came home from that trip and developed her own version of that once famous Lasagna.

RONNIE MURRAY

LASAGNA BY SUSIE

INGREDIENTS

2 pounds ground chuck

1 pound Italian sausage

3 tablespoons minced onion

1 teaspoon garlic powder

¼ teaspoon salt

¼ teaspoon pepper

6 wide lasagna noodles

8 cups shredded mozzarella cheese

3 pounds spaghetti sauce

¼ cup Parmesan cheese

INSTRUCTIONS

Brown ground chuck and Italian sausage with onion in pan. Add salt and pepper, cook until done. Drain off any fat.

Pour spaghetti sauce in large sauce pan, add meat mixture and simmer for 20 minutes. Cook lasagna noodles in boiling water and garlic powder. Cook until done and drain.

Preheat oven to 350°F.

Use a 13x9x2-inch pan and pour some of the spaghetti sauce in the bottom of the pan and cover with noodles.

Add 3 cups of mozzarella cheese and ½ of the Parmesan cheese. Layer sauce, noodles, 3 cups of mozzarella cheese and the rest of the Parmesan cheese.

Pour the remaining spaghetti sauce on top and add the remaining 2 cups of mozzarella cheese.

Bake uncovered for 40 minutes or until browned. Let set for 10 to 15 minutes before serving.

PEOPLE SERVED: 8 TO 12

MAIN DISHES

This has been a go-to weeknight recipe at our house since the kids were small.

It's easy to keep all of the ingredients on hand if chicken is always in your freezer, as it is in ours.

And it's a nice excuse to open a bottle of wine!

BARBARA MOCKETT

CHICKEN IMPERIAL
CHICKEN WITH RICE AND SAUCE

INGREDIENTS

⅓ cup dry wine

1 tablespoon butter

2 teaspoons Worcestershire sauce

1 teaspoon salt

1 teaspoon dried oregano leaves

1 teaspoon curry powder

½ teaspoon dry mustard

½ teaspoon garlic powder

¼ teaspoon paprika

3-4 pound chicken, cut in pieces

4 servings cooked rice, hot

INSTRUCTIONS

Preheat oven to 375°F.

Combine the first nine ingredients (wine through paprika) and heat in a small saucepan, stirring occasionally.

Place chicken pieces in an open 9x13-inch pan. Pour liquid over chicken. Roast in a 375°F. oven for one hour, basting occasionally.

After roasting, place chicken pieces on a plate, pour sauce into a cup and strain off fat. Serve chicken with rice, use sauce on the rice as desired.

PEOPLE SERVED: 4-5

MAIN DISHES

Growing up in Boulder, Colorado,
I was lucky to have a mom that was one of the original health food nuts.

Fried foods were taboo in our household and we usually ate carob in place of chocolate. We also ate Kretschmer wheat germ in just about every recipe that could accommodate it.

This recipe was one of my favorites, because to me it tasted better than fried fast food chicken but it was

"good for you"

and the wheat germ made it "extra crispy" long before it was a fast food option.

TODD NORBY

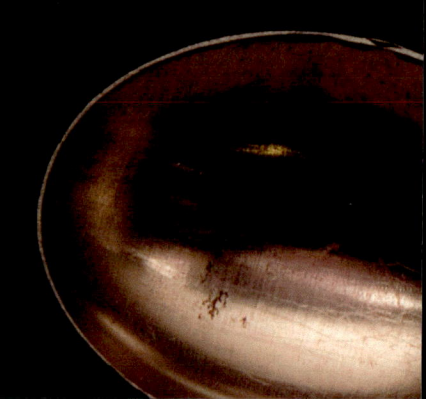

OVEN BAKED CHICKEN

INGREDIENTS

3-4 pounds chicken pieces (drumsticks and thighs turn out best)

1 cup whole wheat flour

½ cup Kretschmer wheat germ

1 egg

1 tablespoon milk

½ teaspoon paprika, adjust to taste

½ teaspoon salt, adjust to taste

½ teaspoon ground black pepper, adjust to taste

1 teaspoon Italian seasoning (or combine your own!)

INSTRUCTIONS

Preheat oven to 375°F.

Lightly grease large 9x13-inch casserole baking pan.

Cut up and clean chicken, remove skin if desired.

Beat egg and blend with milk in a small bowl. In a separate bowl, blend all dry ingredients.

Dip each chicken piece in egg mixture and fully cover with coating. Arrange pieces in greased pan, leaving gaps between each piece.

Bake at 375°F. for 45 minutes, turn each piece, lightly dust with remaining coating and bake an additional 15 minutes until golden brown and juice from the thickest piece is clear (not pink) when cut.

Alternatively, ensure meat has reached 165°F. at the center of the thickest piece.

Replace some of the flour with grated Parmesan for a delicious variant.

PEOPLE SERVED: 4

MAIN DISHES

My roots are in Norway and Alaska,
so you could say salmon is my soul food.

It is the very first thing I remember eating.

I was three or four years old, and our family was living on the banks of the **Taku River in Alaska,** where my father, a fisheries biologist, was studying salmon runs.

The way I season salmon when I bake it today is a departure from my Nordic heritage, but not a huge one. **Like many things Scandinavian,** this recipe is simple and allows the flavor of the fish to come through.

It's the one I love to share with friends and family.

VAL THORSON

SIMPLE BAKED SALMON

INGREDIENTS

1 salmon filet
(allowing 4 to 8 ounces per person, depending on appetites)

1 tablespoon olive oil

1 to 2 tablespoons chopped fresh tarragon

Salt to taste
(I like to use lime salt, which has small bits of dried peel in it.)

Fresh ground black or white pepper

PEOPLE SERVED: 4

INSTRUCTIONS

Preheat oven to 350°F.

Brush a baking pan with olive oil. Brush the flesh side of fish with the rest of the oil and lay it skin side down in the pan.

Sprinkle the tarragon evenly over the salmon. Very lightly salt and grind fresh pepper over it.

Cover the baking dish with foil. Put the fish in the center of your preheated oven. Bake for 15 minutes, then remove the foil.

Look at the fish: it should have a red stripe at the thickest part. Return the fish to the oven, minus the foil, for 2 minutes.

Check the fish again: the red stripe should be nearly, but not completely, gone.

Bake a little longer if necessary, checking frequently.

When there is still a small red stripe (about ½ inch) still visible, take the fish out of the oven.

Let the salmon stand a few minutes while you make a salad or set the table. The heat in the fish will cook it to the perfectly done - but not the least bit overdone - point.

Serve with salad, bread or boiled red potatoes and Pinot Noir or a chilled dry white wine.

MAIN DISHES

This recipe is taken out of my blog: **"Flavor IT with Love"**. If you cook with Love your dishes will speak for itself. My recipes are inspired, infused and tested (or is it tasted!) **with Love!**

I love discovering new flavors, and I constantly experiment with flavors to either bring out a subtle hidden flavor or to round off a dominant flavor.

Feel free to add your **twist of change** to the recipe and share your flavor experience with us.

PREETHA JAYASINGH

MOROCCAN STYLE LAMB ROAST

INGREDIENTS

Fresh lamb leg boneless (2.5 pounds)

Juice and grated peel of 1 orange

½ cup fresh cranberries

2 cups tomato sauce

1 large red onion, chopped

3 cloves garlic, crushed

1 tablespoon coriander powder

1 sprig fresh thyme

1 sprig fresh rosemary

½ cup unsalted butter

Salt to taste

PEOPLE SERVED: 4

INSTRUCTIONS

Preheat oven to 425°F. Place cast iron cookware in oven.

Add about ½ a stick of butter and melt the butter in the oven.

Place the lamb fat-side down and let it cook until the fat starts to melt and the surface of the meat has caramelized to a brown color. (About 15 min).

Remove the lamb from the cast iron cookware. Add chopped onion and crushed garlic to the melted fat in the empty cast iron cookware. Stir and cook in the oven until caramelized (about 15 minutes).

Add tomato sauce and stir. Add the lamb and remaining ingredients.

Cook at 425°F. for 30 minutes. Then turn down the heat to 375°F. and cook for another 2.5 hours.

The lamb should be tender when cut. If not, continue cooking until tender.

ADDITIONAL NOTES

This recipe was birthed as a result of my urge to use up all the ingredients I had left over from my Thanksgiving meal. As an added bonus, Lamb was on sale today!

Lamb has a distinct, strong meaty flavor. I balance the meaty flavor with a citrus top note from oranges and a tart finish from cranberries. Spices and herbs round off the strong flavor of Lamb.

TIDBITS

I use Paula Deen's cast iron cookware.

Cast iron holds and distributes the heat evenly. I love the brown caramelized flavors released when cooking in a cast iron cookware. This recipe can also be done in a crock pot but develops a brothy-herby flavor profile, as opposed to the brown caramelized flavor from the cast iron.

I serve this dish with "Herbed Basmati Rice" and "Roasted Garlic-Asparagus".

Wine Pairing: Best served with Cabernet Sauvignon or Merlot.

This recipe was handed down from my granny (great-gramma). It was a popular meal during the Great Depression.

It's a **favorite dish** in my family.

RACHYL MILLER

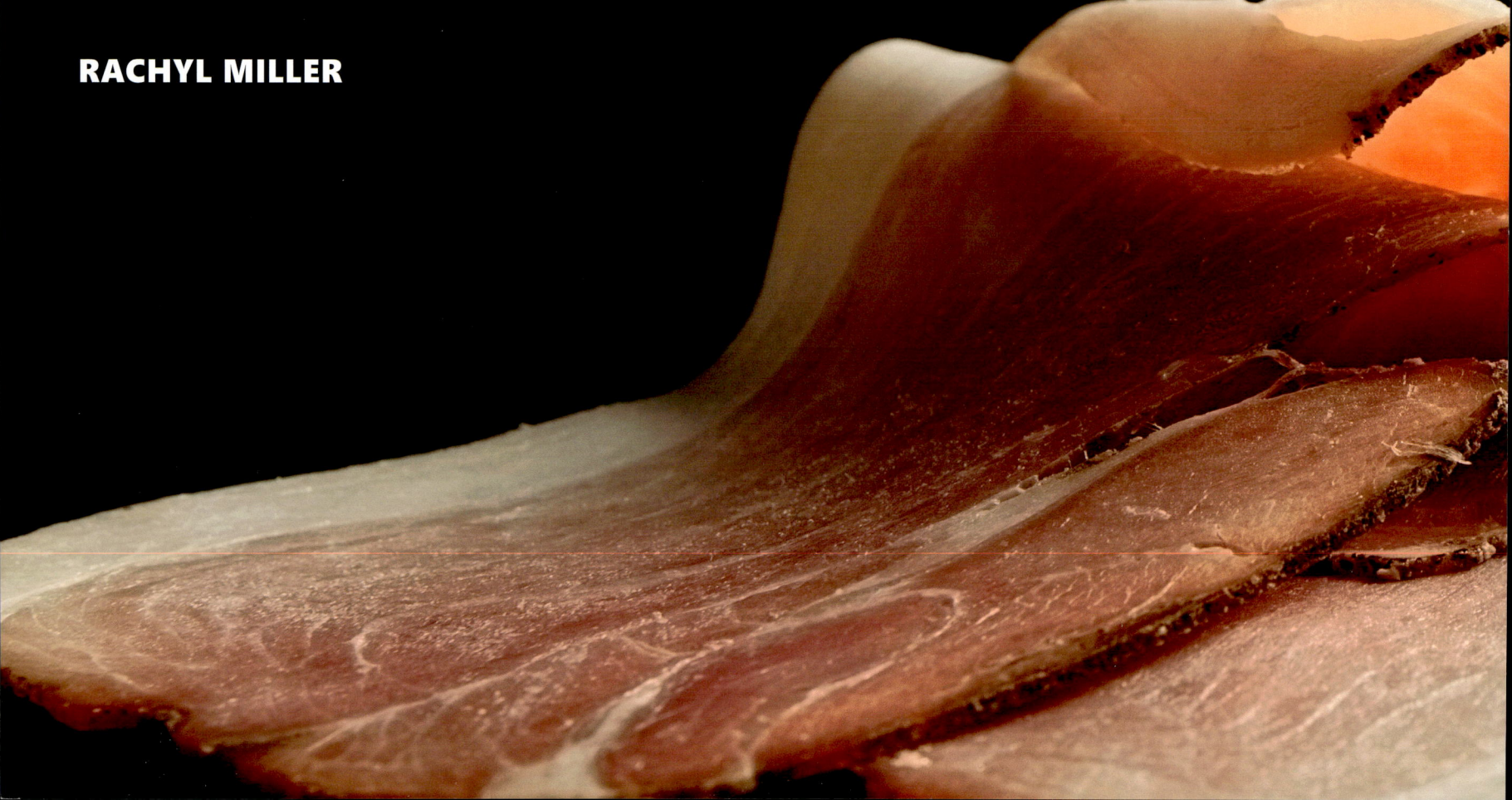

GREAT GRAMMA'S BACON NOODLES

INGREDIENTS

1 pound bacon

16 ounces cottage cheese

16 ounces sour cream

16 ounce bag egg noodles (bow-ties work well too)

Salt & pepper to taste

PEOPLE SERVED: 8

INSTRUCTIONS

Cut bacon into approximately 1 inch strips, cook and drain. Set aside.

In a separate pot, bring water to a boil and cook egg noodles. Drain.

Once the noodles and bacon are done, mix remaining ingredients into the noodles, leaving the stove on low heat. Mix thoroughly, add bacon, seasoning salt and pepper.

Let it continue to warm for approximately 5 minutes, stirring a couple of times.

Serve and enjoy!

MAIN DISHES

This recipe is something I basically made up in order to "impress" my parents after I moved out on my own and invited them over for the **first home cooked meal** of mine.

I've made changes and substitutions to it over the years. You can add more spices to kick up the flavor and use canned crab meat or tuna in place of the shrimp.

It's very **simple** but simply **delicious**.

TIFFANY LUBY

EASY PASTA WITH SHRIMP

INGREDIENTS

½ pound angel hair pasta - or shape of your choice

½ cup extra virgin olive oil

2 garlic cloves, minced

½ cup onion, minced

1 - 14.5 ounce can diced tomatoes or 2 cups fresh tomatoes, diced

½ cup mushrooms, sliced

¼ cup fresh basil, chopped

8-12 ounces medium shrimp, cooked and peeled

Grated Parmesan cheese

INSTRUCTIONS

Cook pasta in boiling water until al dente.

Meanwhile heat olive oil in skillet and sauté garlic, onion and mushrooms for about 5 minutes.

Add tomatoes and basil and simmer for about 5 minutes. Add shrimp and cook until heated through.

Pour sauce over pasta and top with grated Parmesan cheese.

Enjoy!

PEOPLE SERVED: 2-4

SIDE DISHES

SIDE DISHES

I learned to cook from my Grandmother Amina who was born in Kashmir, in the northwestern region of India. My grandfather was an English language teacher during the time of British occupied India. After they were married, my grandparents lived in Dehradun at the foot of the Himalayan Mountains nestled between two mighty rivers: the Ganges and the Yamuna. This picturesque valley was rich in wild life.

My grandfather was the proverbial "hunter, gatherer". On his way home from work, through the forested area, on a bicycle, he would carry his gun and actually kill something for dinner.

My grandmother would never know if it was going to be a duck, a pheasant, a fish or even a deer. Being a resourceful woman, she always kept a small basket of potatoes around in her kitchen, for those occasions when there were no surprises for dinner.

Her spicy potatoes were a favorite family recipe that my daughters and I still enjoy.

SAMINA VAN WINKLE

AMINA'S SPICY POTATOES

INGREDIENTS

3 pounds of new potatoes red or white, chopped in roughly 2 inch cubes

1 tablespoon coriander powder

1 tablespoon cumin powder

2 or 3 dried cayenne whole peppers

1 teaspoon cayenne

1 teaspoon paprika

¼ teaspoon turmeric, ground

1 teaspoon ginger powder

2 teaspoons cumin seed

1 tablespoon garlic, crushed

1 medium onion, chopped

4 tablespoons olive oil

2 medium tomatoes, chopped

½ cup cilantro, chopped

Salt to taste

PEOPLE SERVED: 4-6

INSTRUCTIONS

Mix potatoes and all spices except garlic and cumin seed in a large bowl. Make sure that the potatoes are well coated evenly.

In a pan large enough for the potatoes, heat olive oil (medium heat) and add cumin seed and stir until seeds look toasted red brown. This can happen in about 30 seconds to 1 minute in hot oil. Don't burn the cumin seeds as they will become bitter.

Add garlic and chopped onion and stir until onions are a little transparent but not brown (about a minute). Add potatoes and chopped tomatoes, and stir well to mix everything.

Cover the pan and lower the heat. Allow to cook on low heat for about 45 minutes depending on the type of potato and the size of the pieces.

Check potatoes after 30 minutes, if the potatoes are sticking add a quarter cup of water. Test with a fork or a toothpick to see if they are close to being done. Cook to the consistency desired. Potatoes should be soft but still retain some shape.

Before serving pick out and throw away the whole cayenne peppers and garnish with chopped cilantro.

SIDE DISHES

Green Bean Bundles are a holiday favorite at our house.

My sister got this recipe many years ago from a friend of hers who was the Culinary Arts teacher at our local school.

We have had Green Bean Bundles every Thanksgiving and Christmas since, and there are never any left.

I usually have to make two or three batches to have enough to go around.

MELISSA NICHOLS

GREEN BEAN BUNDLES

INGREDIENTS

4 cans whole green beans, drained

Thin sliced bacon, cut slices in half

Garlic pepper

½ cup brown sugar

½ cup butter

INSTRUCTIONS

Heat oven to 375°F.

Spray ½ sheet (about 10x15-inches) or 9x13-inch baking pan with vegetable spray.

Drain green beans. Take five or six whole green beans and wrap with ½ slice bacon. Place on sheet pan.

Melt butter in sauce pan and add brown sugar and stir until well mixed.

Drizzle brown sugar mixture over bundles and sprinkle with garlic pepper.

Bake at 375°F. for approximately 45 minutes or until desired doneness of the bacon.

PEOPLE SERVED: 4-6

SIDE DISHES

This is one of our **favorite side dishes** to serve when grilling steak, chicken, pork or any other grilled main course.

These are so good that we "**jockey**" for the leftovers...if there are any!

I love them so much, that I have made a meal out of just the potatoes – *forget the meat!*

Enjoy!

BECKY KELLEY

TWICE AS NICE BAKED POTATOES

INGREDIENTS

3 large baking potatoes

2 tablespoons softened butter

¾ teaspoon salt

1 - 2 tablespoons diced green onion

1 ½ cups grated sharp cheddar cheese, divided

2 egg yolks

½ cup sour cream

INSTRUCTIONS

Wash and dry potatoes. Poke potatoes with fork. Wrap in foil and bake at 350°F. for 90 minutes or until done.

Halve the potatoes lengthwise. Carefully scoop out the pulp, reserving the skins.

Mash the potato pulp with butter while still hot. Add salt, green onion and ½ cup grated cheese.

Blend egg yolks and sour cream and add to potato mixture. Fill potato skins with potato mixture.

Top potatoes with remaining grated cheese. Place potatoes on preheated grill (medium indirect heat) and cook 20 minutes.

PEOPLE SERVED: MAKES 6 SERVINGS

SIDE DISHES

When I was a kid I spent my summers in **Mexico. I loved going to the markets and parks lined with vendors** of almost anything you can think of. My favorite was the elote. It was as beautiful as cotton candy at a fair.

The corn is sweet and the chili is hot but you can't stop eating it, it's so good!

MARLENA AGUINIGA

MEXICAN ELOTE
(CORN ON THE COB)

INGREDIENTS

4 ears of corn, roasted or boiled

1 lime, cut in half

Mayonnaise

Queso cotija, grated or Parmesan cheese

Pico de gallo chili powder or cayenne pepper powder

INSTRUCTIONS

Roast the corn to your preferred doneness. When cool enough to handle peel back the leaves to create a handle. If boiled, add a cob holder on the end.

Holding the corn by the handle, squeeze/rub lime juice all over the corn. Then spread a thin layer of mayonnaise all over the corn. Now, sprinkle the cheese all over the corn to coat it.

Finally, add the chili powder to your taste.

PEOPLE SERVED: 4

SIDE DISHES

I grew up in the Renton Highlands and for as long as I can remember the hydroplane races ran on Lake Washington the first Sunday in August.

My family would look forward to having a barbecue and watching the races on TV – *we would even take the TV set outside and hook up the antenna so that we could be out in the sun.*

My mom used to make these beans every year and it wasn't hydro race day without them.

For my family they are more than just baked beans - **they are memories of the wonderful times we have had as a family** over the years and of the grandparents who are no longer with us.

JOANNE HEINEMAN

VERDA'S BAKED BEANS

INGREDIENTS

2 - 28 ounce cans baked beans

1 cup diced onions

½ cup dark molasses

¾ cup brown sugar

1 teaspoon mustard

Dash of cayenne

Dash of ground cloves

½ cup ketchup - or to taste

INSTRUCTIONS

Mix all ingredients together in a bean pot.

Bake at 350°F. for 2 to 3 hours.

PEOPLE SERVED: 8-10

SIDE DISHES

My parents are wonderful gardeners. They honor us every Christmas with 2 dozen quarts of home canned green beans. **They are amazing.**

This recipe is one of my favorite ways to enjoy them. I call it **Jerusalem Green Beans** because that is where I first tasted this healthy goodness.

Serve this with rice, warm pita or very crusty artisan bread. If you have meat eaters in the family add roasted cubed lamb or stew meat.

This is a wonderful make-ahead dish; **the flavors are even better the next day.**

MALIA HASEGAWA

JERUSALEM GREEN BEANS

INGREDIENTS

1 pound green beans with ends trimmed, halved, OR 1 quart canned beans

1 onion, chopped

⅓ cup olive oil

3 cloves garlic, crushed or minced fine

1 - 28-ounce can chopped tomatoes, drained

½ teaspoon salt

¼ teaspoon pepper

¼ teaspoon ground allspice

Pinch of sugar, optional

INSTRUCTIONS

In a large sauce pan, cook the onions in olive oil until they take on a bit of color. Add the green beans. Let them brighten and the onions brown, then add the garlic.

Heat thoroughly, adding the tomatoes, salt, pepper and allspice. Cover. Check them after 15-20 minutes; continue cooking based on your preference. (I like my beans with a bit of crispness, although the more authentic recipes tend toward "well done.")

This is excellent hot, lukewarm, cool, or next day.

PEOPLE SERVED: WILL YIELD ABOUT TWO HEALTHY SERVINGS FOR A MAIN DISH, OR FOUR AS A SIDE.

What Idaho girl wasn't raised on Idaho Potatoes?

In the area I grew up it was known as the Potato Capital of the World. *OK, so we like to exaggerate a bit.*

My **great grandfather** was one of the first residents to establish a little town called Parker Idaho.

There they raised livestock and farmed wheat and potatoes on what they called "Dry Farms". This was before they had irrigation and the only water the crops received was from the rain. He was one of the first to grow what is now called Russet Burbank Potatoes in the early 1900s.

This is my favorite recipe - Smashed Potato Gratin, or in my family *Smashed Cheese Potatoes* recipe, as it goes as a side dish with any meal.

It is a staple at our house for big family gatherings.

ERIN EDLEFSEN

SMASHED POTATO GRATIN

INGREDIENTS

3 pounds Idaho russet potatoes

3 garlic cloves, peeled

Kosher salt

1 cup milk

1 cup sour cream

2 cups grated cheddar cheese

¾ cup panko bread crumbs

½ cup grated Parmesan cheese

Pinch cayenne pepper

1 bunch chives

PEOPLE SERVED: 12

INSTRUCTIONS

Peel potatoes, then cut into quarters and place in a large saucepan with the garlic. Fill the pot with water and season generously with salt. Taste the water, it should taste salty.

Bring the pot to a boil over medium heat and cook the potatoes until they are fork tender. (A fork, not a knife, should slide in and out easily.)

Preheat oven to 350°F.

When the potatoes are tender, drain the water from them and return the potatoes and garlic to the pan.

Add the milk and sour cream. Using a potato masher or a big spoon, gently mash the potatoes. Stir in the cheddar cheese, and then taste and season with salt if needed. (With the salted water more might not be necessary.)

Transfer the mixture into a baking dish. Combine the panko bread crumbs, grated Parmesan cheese and the cayenne in a small bowl.

Sprinkle it over the top of the potato mixture and bake until hot all the way through and crispy and brown on top, about 20 minutes.

Remove from the oven, garnish with chopped chives and serve.

SIDE DISHES

MOM'S *"EVERYONE'S TOGETHER"* BROCCOLI & RICE CASSEROLE

INGREDIENTS

- 1 small onion
- 2 tablespoons butter
- 2 - 10 ounce packages of frozen broccoli
- 1 - 10.75 ounce can cream of chicken soup
- ½ cup milk
- 1 cup Minute rice, cooked
- ½ pound Velveeta cheese, cut into 1" squares

INSTRUCTIONS

Chop the onion and sauté in butter over medium heat until translucent.

Cook broccoli until just thawed and drain.

Mix together all ingredients and place in a lightly greased 2 quart casserole dish.

Bake at 350°F. for 30 minutes.

PEOPLE SERVED: 6-8

This recipe has been a family staple for as long as I can remember.

Every time the family is together, whether it is for holidays or birthdays, **my Mom makes this casserole.**

Best of all, everyone enjoys this dish, especially my boys!

KEN MOYER

SIDE DISHES

I developed this recipe for the first Continental Mills Harvest Potluck that I attended.

We do love to have fun here, and **good eating** is a big part of the fun!

Butternut Squash is roasted under a broiler, giving it a unique "blackened" appearance.

The flavor of the squash is enhanced with the addition of crisp cooked bacon, grilled onion, and warm sweet spices.

AMY STONE

ROASTED BUTTERNUT SQUASH

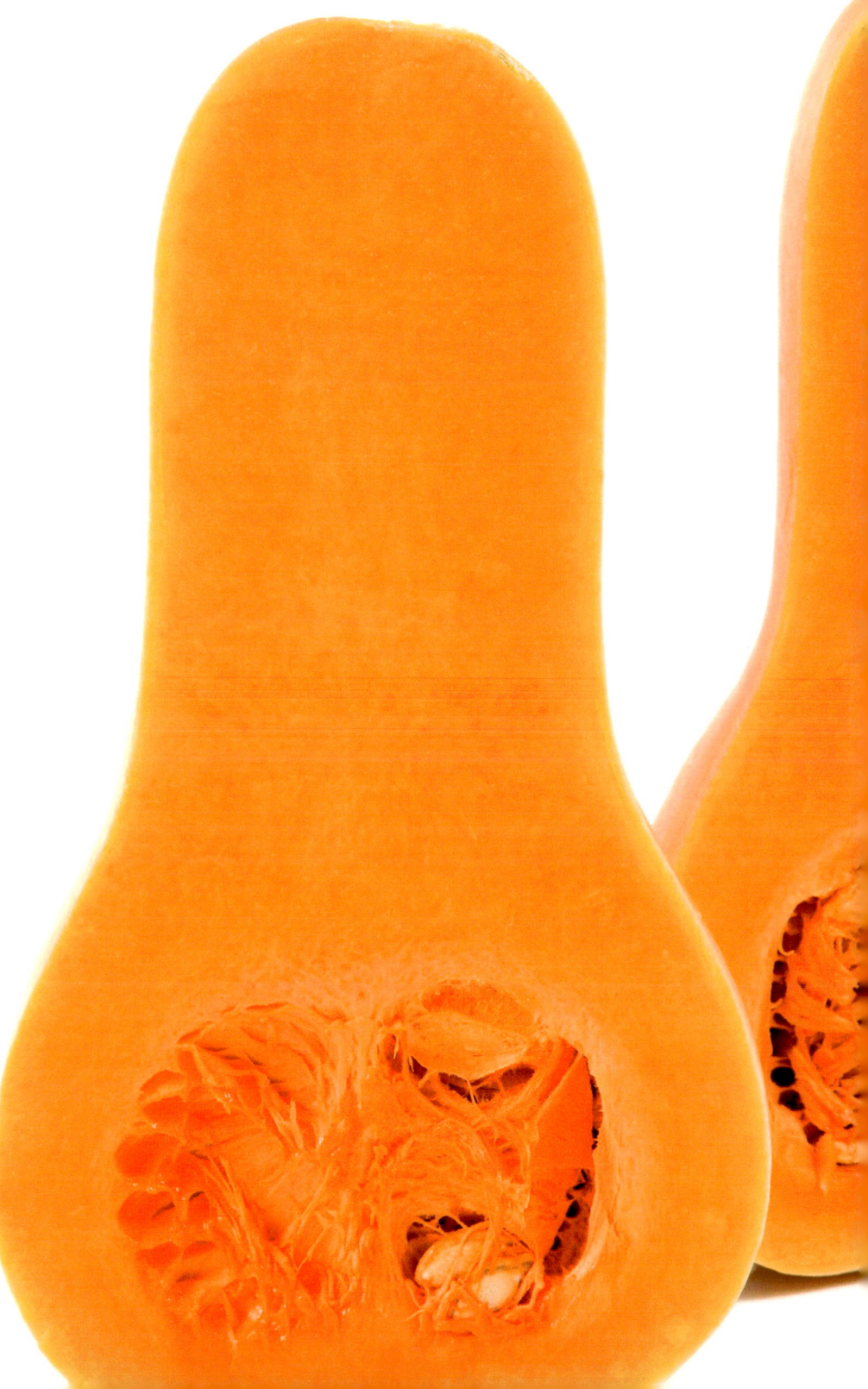

INGREDIENTS

2 large butternut squash, peeled and cubed

¼ cup butter

¾ pound sliced bacon, cut into ¼ inch pieces

½ onion, cubed

⅔ cup brown sugar

1 ⅛ teaspoons salt

½ teaspoon cinnamon

⅛ teaspoon nutmeg

INSTRUCTIONS

In frying pan, brown bacon and onion together. Drain excess fat and set aside.

Combine brown sugar, salt, cinnamon and nutmeg. Set aside.

Melt butter in roasting pan. Add squash cubes and coat with butter. Broil until edges of squash begin to brown, turning frequently with a spatula. Squash will be done when tender, but still holds its shape. Do not overcook.

Toss with bacon and sugar mixture. Return to oven until squash begins to sizzle.

Transfer to serving bowl and serve hot.

PEOPLE SERVED: 12

SIDE DISHES

In the northwest we've learned what grows and what doesn't. **The zucchini plant is undoubtedly the most prolific producer in the vegetable garden.** Growing up we had plants that produced so much that we looked for any way to incorporate them into a meal.

If you don't check your plants daily you end up with a zucchini the size of a small boat. **My mother made a dish that we nicknamed "zucchini boat"** - which was really meatloaf baked in a hollowed out zucchini that had gone unnoticed in the garden.

I prefer harvesting them when they are about six inches long and using them in this zucchini bake.

NAOMI MCKAY

ZUCCHINI BAKE

INGREDIENTS

1 tablespoon olive oil

1 red pepper, diced

1 sweet onion, diced

4 cloves fresh garlic, minced

4-6 zucchini, diced

Salt and pepper to taste

10 ounces fresh spinach

1 ½ cups marinara sauce (homemade or store bought)

½ cup fresh basil, chopped

16 ounces polenta, plain or seasoned, sliced lengthwise into 6 equal portions

1 ½ cups Parmesan cheese

INSTRUCTIONS

Heat oil in large skillet over medium-high heat.

Sauté pepper, onion, garlic and zucchini, until just tender.

Add spinach and cook until wilted, stirring occasionally. Add marinara sauce and stir together. Remove from heat and add basil.

Place sliced polenta in lightly sprayed 9X13-inch baking dish. Sprinkle 1 cup of Parmesan cheese over the polenta.

Top with zucchini mixture and sprinkle with remaining Parmesan cheese.

Bake at 450°F. for 10-15 minutes, let stand for 5 minutes before serving.

PEOPLE SERVED: 8

DESSERTS

DESSERTS

Did you know that Washington State has one of the best climates for growing raspberries?

My mother-in-law, also known as Grandma Tish, must have known this fact because she not only grew raspberries in her garden; she would also make and freeze raspberry jam, raspberry juice and whole raspberries so that she could **enjoy them all** year long.

And remember raspberries not only **taste great,** they are truly a part of Washington's agricultural community.

Please **enjoy and think of Grandma "Tish"** when you make this recipe.

CYNTHIA SASAKI

RED AND WHITE LAYERED RASPBERRY PIE

INGREDIENTS

1 - 3 ounce package raspberry flavored gelatin

¼ cup sugar

1 ¼ cups boiling water

1 - 12 ounce package frozen red raspberries

1 tablespoon lemon juice

1 - 4 ounce package cream cheese, softened

½ cup powdered sugar, sifted

1 teaspoon vanilla

½ pint whipping cream, whipped

Dash salt

1 - 9-inch baked pastry shell cooled or 9-inch graham cracker pie crust

Optional: Fresh Northwest raspberries as garnish or additional whipping cream

INSTRUCTIONS

RED LAYERS:

Dissolve gelatin and granulated sugar in boiling water. Add frozen berries and lemon juice. Stir until berries are thawed. Chill until partially set.

WHITE LAYERS:

Blend softened cream cheese and sifted powdered sugar together. Add vanilla and salt. Fold in a small amount of the whipped cream. Then fold in the remainder of the whipped cream.

FILLING PIE SHELL:

Spread one half of the white cream cheese mixture over the bottom of the pastry or graham cracker pie crust. Cover the white layer with one half of red gelatin mixture. Repeat layers. Chill until set.

GARNISH:

You can always add fresh raspberries to the top of the pie and more whipping cream!

PEOPLE SERVED: 6-8

I grew up on a farm in rural Eastern Colorado. Food and agriculture were a huge part of my childhood, including participating in 4-H, a youth organization that was very popular in our community. I was in the baking group of 4-H, and entered this sugar cookie recipe into the Colorado State Fair in 1981...

and won STATE Grand Champion!

However, there was a scandal!

The cookies were not allowed to be formed with cookie cutters, and my cookies looked perfectly round because of the way you press them down with the bottom of a greased, sugared glass.

One of the moms of another girl whose cookies didn't win was jealous and accused me of cheating!

Everyone knew that my cookies were legitimate (*including the 4-H judges*) and **we still have a good laugh over the story every time we make them.**

'GRAND CHAMPION' SUGAR COOKIES

INGREDIENTS & INSTRUCTIONS

Large Bowl #1:

Beat the following ingredients until light and fluffy:

1 cup shortening (½ butter and ½ Crisco solid shortening)

1 cup powdered sugar, sifted

Add the following ingredients to the mixture:

1 egg, beaten

1 teaspoon vanilla

PEOPLE SERVED:

MAKES APPROXIMATELY 3 DOZEN

Medium Bowl #2

2 cups flour

½ teaspoon salt

½ teaspoon cream of tartar

½ teaspoon baking soda

Mix well and add to ingredients in bowl #1. Chill and roll into balls (approximately walnut size). With a greased, flat glass bottom dipped in granulated sugar, flatten each ball (may use colored sugar).

Bake at 375°F. for 8-10 minutes or until light golden brown.

DESSERTS

When I think of the holidays I think of these cookies.

This was my nana's recipe and every year for over 20 years we would make these together.

With family traveling from all over the country to get together once a year, these cookies were always in high demand and never lasted long. **It was very common that I and other grandkids would have to talk nana into cooking a second batch with us.**

My family has been enjoying these shortbread cookies for years and I hope your family will do the same.

REBECCA JOHNSTON

NANA'S THUMBPRINT COOKIES

INGREDIENTS

Cookie Dough:

½ cup butter

1 teaspoon vanilla

1 ½ cups flour

½ cup brown sugar, packed

½ teaspoon salt

2 tablespoons milk

¼ cup chopped chocolate chips

Powdered sugar
(used for coating cookies once baked)

Chocolate Filling:

¾ cup chocolate chips

1 tablespoon shortening

2 tablespoons white corn syrup

1 tablespoon water

1 teaspoon vanilla

INSTRUCTIONS

Preheat oven to 375°F.

Cream ½ cup butter with ½ teaspoon salt and 1 teaspoon vanilla; add ½ cup packed brown sugar. Blend in 1 ½ cups flour, 2 tablespoons milk, and ¼ cup chopped chocolate chips.

With your hands roll dough into 1 inch balls and place on ungreased cookie sheet. Make a thumb print in the center of the dough ball for your filling. (Little thumbs work just as well as big thumbs).

Bake 10-12 minutes. Cookies will be slightly golden. Place powdered sugar on plate and while cookies are still warm roll in powdered sugar to evenly coat.

Allow to cool, and then fill with chocolate filling.

Chocolate Filling:

Over hot, not boiling, water melt ¾ cup chocolate chips with 1 tablespoon shortening. Stir until melted.

Cool slightly then stir in 2 tablespoons white corn syrup, 1 tablespoon water, and 1 teaspoon vanilla.

Use spoon to fill cooled center of cookies immediately while filling is still warm.

Allow filled cookies to cool completely before serving.

PEOPLE SERVED: 3 DOZEN

DESSERTS

My family has always baked at Christmas time and one of our favorites is my mom's Chocolate Fudge (passed down from my grandmother).

When my ship was stationed in Bahrain during the first Gulf War my parents kept me and my shipmates in the Christmas mood by sending multiple shipments of this fudge. **It was one of those simple things that meant a lot to me and my friends during a stressful time.**

Now when I **bake with my son,** I tell him how his grandparents made one Christmas a little more special for me.

MATTHEW WEISE

MOM'S CHOCOLATE FUDGE

INGREDIENTS

1 - 12 ounce can evaporated milk

4 ½ cups sugar

24 ounces semi-sweet chocolate chips

16 ounce milk chocolate candy bar

2 pints marshmallow crème

1 teaspoon vanilla extract

¼ pound butter

2 pounds walnuts (optional)

INSTRUCTIONS

Add milk and sugar to a large pot and continue stirring until it comes to a boil. Boil for 5 minutes and remove from heat.

Stir in all other ingredients except for butter and nuts. Stir until they are mixed thoroughly then add butter and nuts.

Stir until all is melted. Pour quickly into a buttered pan. We have found that a broiling pan works best.

PEOPLE SERVED: 1 TO 50

Almost any fiesta in my hometown of Pateros, Philippines, is celebrated with lots of activities and lots of good food.

From the traditional dishes and delightful desserts that everyone looks forward to savoring during the celebration, my mother's leche flan has its own special place on the table.

Growing up, I had to help her make this sweet delicacy two to three days before the event. It is included in the planning to cook so much more than necessary because,

Dorie, my dear loving mother, is more than happy to indulge friends and family who would request to take home some of her flan.

We all now live here in the USA but **we still keep the tradition** of cooking extra for giveaways.

ALITHA EDWARDS

DORIE'S LECHE FLAN

INGREDIENTS

1 cup granulated sugar

1 tablespoon water

8 egg yolks

1 egg white

1 cup whole milk
(2% or non-fat or coconut milk are okay too)

1 - 14 ounce can condensed milk

1 teaspoon vanilla extract

INSTRUCTIONS

Melt 1 cup sugar and 1 tablespoon of water in a saucepan until golden brown. Immediately pour into the bottom and sides of the 1 quart mold or llanera that will be used to steam or bake the flan mixture.

In a mixing bowl, mix well all remaining ingredients, then pour into the mold container lined with caramel.

Traditional cooking method is by steaming covered for about 30 minutes or until mixture is set. Another cooking method is to put mold in a water bath. Bake for 1 hour or until set at 350°F. Cool for about 30 minutes before removing from the mold container.

Serve with toasted coconut on the side, or whatever berries that are in season.

Sliced almonds sprinkled on top of the leche flan is another way to present it.

Optional:

1 tablespoon of lemon or lime zest to be added to the flan mixture prior to steaming or baking.

PEOPLE SERVED: 6 TO 8

DESSERTS

My family enjoys this tasty treat every Christmas!

It is easy to make and gives your **home a sweet and spicy aroma as it bakes!**

SUSAN ENGDAHL

SOPAPILLA CHEESECAKE BARS

INGREDIENTS

2 - 8 ounce packages cream cheese, softened

1 cup white sugar

1 teaspoon vanilla extract

2 - 8 ounce cans refrigerated crescent rolls

¾ cup white sugar

1 teaspoon ground cinnamon

½ cup butter, room temperature

¼ cup honey

PEOPLE SERVED: 12

INSTRUCTIONS

Preheat an oven to 350°F.

Prepare a 9x13-inch baking dish with cooking spray.

Beat the cream cheese with 1 cup of sugar and the vanilla extract in a bowl until smooth.

Unroll the cans of crescent roll dough, and use a rolling pin to shape each piece into 9x13-inch rectangles. Press one piece into the bottom of a 9x13-inch baking dish.

Evenly spread the cream cheese mixture into the baking dish, then cover with the remaining piece of crescent dough.

Stir together ¾ cup of sugar, cinnamon, and butter. Drizzle the mixture over the top of the cheesecake.

Bake in the preheated oven until the crescent dough has puffed and turned golden brown, about 30 minutes. Remove from the oven and drizzle with honey. Cool completely in the pan before cutting into 12 squares.

DESSERTS

This recipe is a makeover from **one of my favorite food shows.**

I changed some of the ingredients to suit my taste. I enjoy remaking recipes to see what different combinations I can make. **This is one of the reasons I am well-nourished (fluffy).**

This is a great recipe for summertime.

I hope you will **enjoy it.**

JOANN GREEN

SUMMER TIME ICE CREAM TREAT

INGREDIENTS

1 - 14.3 ounce package round chocolate sandwich cookies, crushed

1 - 1.5 quart snickers ice cream, softened

3 bananas, sliced

Hot fudge topping for ice cream

Caramel topping for ice cream

1 - 8 ounce container whipped topping, thawed

½ cup nuts, chopped

1 - 10 ounce jar Maraschino cherries

INSTRUCTIONS

Layer ingredients in 13X9-inch pan as follows:

Crushed cookies, softened ice cream, sliced bananas, drizzle hot fudge & caramel topping, Spread on whipped topping, drizzle hot fudge & caramel topping, top with nuts & cherries.

Keep frozen until ready to enjoy.

PEOPLE SERVED: 6-8

I grew up on a farm (the same farm my father grew up on) in Southeast Wisconsin. It was a self-sustaining farm and all of our food was grown and harvested on it.

We had apple orchards...Wolf River apple trees. My four siblings and I had to climb trees and pick all the apples. *We picked apples all day and threw the rotten ones at each other.*

My mom made Apple Crunch every day in the fall and I would help her. **I remember one time I picked the biggest apple we had ever seen and it made one entire Apple Crunch.**

My mom never had a written recipe... they were all stored in her head. **Last Christmas,** *I made her write every recipe down (over 60).* I made a cookbook for the entire extended family to enjoy for years to come.

Lots of wonderful memories...
I hope you enjoy it!

KELLY DUFFIN-MAXWELL

APPLE CRUNCH

INGREDIENTS

6-7 apples, sliced

½ cup white sugar

1 teaspoon cinnamon (a little more or a little less, depending on what you like)

1 cup flour

1 cup brown sugar

½ cup (1 stick) butter

PEOPLE SERVED: 4-6

INSTRUCTIONS

Place apples into buttered 8x8-inch pan. Cover with white sugar. Sprinkle with cinnamon.

Mix flour, brown sugar and butter until crumbly.

Pour over apples and bake one hour at 325°F.

Serve warm.

DESSERTS

This cake is the **number one request for birthday celebrations in our family.**

GRANDMA NITA'S CHOCOLATE DESSERT

INGREDIENTS

1 angel food cake mix

1 - 12 ounce package chocolate chips

4 egg yolks

4 tablespoons sugar

4 egg whites

2 ½ pints whipping cream

INSTRUCTIONS

Cook cake mix according to directions and let it cool.

Melt chocolate chips in top of double boiler until chocolate is melted and warm, but not too hot.

In the meantime, combine the sugar and egg yolks and add to the melted chocolate. Heat together well.

Remove chocolate mixture from heat and beat egg whites until stiff. Fold beaten egg whites into chocolate mixture. Beat whipping cream and fold into chocolate mixture also.

Break angel food cake into small pieces and cover bottom of angel food cake pan, then pour some chocolate sauce over cake pieces, continue to layer until all of cake and sauce are used. Gently press down so that cake and sauce are well mixed together.

Place in refrigerator and allow to sit overnight. Once set, invert onto cake plate and spread chocolate sauce to cover cake.

PEOPLE SERVED: 8 - 10

It's a simple, light dessert, but every time we make it, they eat every bite. This is the one dessert we serve that has no leftovers!

TAMI TAYLOR

Every time I make this recipe I am reminded of **my mother.**

She used to make these for me when I was a little girl.

I loved coming home from school and smelling these cookies in the kitchen.

I can remember not having the patience to wait for them to set. My brother and I would scrape them off the wax paper and **eat them while they were hot.**

TAMI TAYLOR

CHOCOLATE PEANUT BUTTER NO BAKE COOKIES

INGREDIENTS

2 cups sugar

½ cup milk

½ cup butter

4 tablespoons cocoa

½ cup creamy peanut butter

2 teaspoons vanilla

3 cups dry quick-cooking oats

INSTRUCTIONS

In a heavy saucepan bring first four ingredients to a boil. Boil for 1 minute, remove from heat and add peanut butter and vanilla.

Mix in the oats and drop by spoonful onto wax paper.

Let cool until set.

PEOPLE SERVED: 24 COOKIES

DESSERTS

Pies were my grandmother's specialty, and this was one of the best - especially when the strawberries were fresh from the garden.

I can recall the meticulous way she went through the berries, finding the most perfectly formed and correctly sized ones, placing them precisely in concentric circles.

Even the pie crust was a work of art, and I can recall some of her pie crust lessons to this day.

For instance, according to my grandmother...

"A girl wasn't ready to get married until she could make a perfectly round pie crust".

TAMMY BARR

FRESH STRAWBERRY PIE

INGREDIENTS

4 cups strawberries

1 cup sugar (if strawberries are very ripe and sweet, the sugar can be reduced to ¾ cup)

¼ teaspoon salt

3 tablespoons cornstarch

1 tablespoon lemon juice

1 whole pie crust

INSTRUCTIONS

Wash and hull 4 cups fresh strawberries and drain thoroughly.

Set aside 2 cups of whole berries. Crush remaining berries in a saucepan.

Mix sugar, salt and cornstarch - add to the crushed berries. Heat, stirring constantly and cook until the mixture thickens.

Remove from heat and stir in lemon juice. Cool.

Spread a small amount of this sauce to cover the bottom of an 8-inch pre-baked pie shell.

Arrange the 2 cups of whole berries in the pie shell and cover with the remaining sauce.

Chill pie until firm. When ready to serve, top with whipped cream or prepared topping.

PEOPLE SERVED: 12

DESSERTS

Holiday gatherings in Pennsylvania as a kid included my grandmother's cake. She would make extra frosting and store it in bowls for the kids to eat with a spoon.

Gotta love grandmas.

I tried the store bought mixes but nothing ever compared to how hers would taste. Then a coworker had a recipe for the frosting and it was great. **Now when I make this I always think of my grandma and my coworker.**

The coworker died in 2008 due to cancer and **the lunchroom in Manhattan, Kansas is dedicated to his memory.**

Thanks Bruce...

TODD RUSSELL

CHOCOLATE CAKE WITH MAPLE FROSTING

INGREDIENTS

Cake Mix:

2 cups sugar

2 cups flour

1 ½ cups cocoa

1 egg

1 tablespoon baking soda

½ teaspoon salt

1 teaspoon vanilla

1 cup vegetable oil

1 cup sour milk
(mix 1 tablespoon of vinegar in milk and let stand)

Maple Frosting:

5 tablespoons flour

1 cup milk

½ teaspoon salt

1 cup shortening

1 cup sugar

1 teaspoon vanilla

2 teaspoons maple flavoring

INSTRUCTIONS

Cake Mix:

Mix all ingredients into a large bowl.

Boil 1 cup of water and add to mix.

Bake at 350°F. for 35 minutes in a greased 9x13-inch pan (not floured).

Maple Frosting:

Mix all ingredients in a sauce pan at medium heat until your desired texture is reached, about 5 minutes.

PEOPLE SERVED: 6

My mom is a master baker of pies!

Our family often tells her that she needs to open her own pie shop. For as long as I can remember, my mom has baked this amazing apple pie during the holidays. It is something our family looks forward to every year!

This recipe is very special to me because it was passed down to my mom from my grandma Laurita, who passed away 8 years ago. **Every year, my mom prepares it with love for our family.**

It makes me very happy to contribute this recipe to the CM cookbook in honor of my mom, Linda, and my grandma - two amazing women for whom I have the upmost admiration and love.

I hope this recipe will bring your families as much joy as it has brought to mine throughout the years.

Enjoy!

JEN SMITH

LINDA'S APPLE PIE

INGREDIENTS

Flaky Pie Crust Ingredients:

1 teaspoon salt

3 cups flour

1 ¼ cups shortening

5 tablespoons water

1 tablespoon white vinegar

1 egg

Pie Filling Ingredients:

6 to 8 cooking apples (preferably Golden Delicious), peeled and thickly sliced (should equal approximately 8 cups)

1 tablespoon lemon juice (optional), use only if you want the apples to be more tart

1 cup sugar

2 tablespoons flour

1 teaspoon ground cinnamon

Dash nutmeg

2 tablespoons butter, cut into small pieces

Milk (to lightly coat pie crust)

Sugar (to sprinkle on top of pie)

PEOPLE SERVED: 8

INSTRUCTIONS

Crust Directions:

Mix together water, white vinegar and egg. Place in refrigerator to chill.

Mix flour and salt together.

Add shortening to flour mixture. Cut in half of shortening first, gently, with fingers; then cut in the remaining shortening.

Make a well in the flour mixture and add the chilled water, vinegar and egg mixture. Gently blend with a fork first then knead and separate into 2 balls of dough. Do not over-handle crust or it will become tough and lose flakiness.

Pie Directions:

Preheat oven to 400°F.

Roll each pie crust dough ball into a circle and press the first circle into a 9" pie plate. Trim dough to ½" beyond the edge of the pie plate.

If desired, sprinkle apples with lemon juice.

Combine sugar, flour, cinnamon and nutmeg in a small bowl. Sprinkle the mixture over the apples and toss until the apples are evenly coated.

Fill the lined pie plate with the apple mixture. Dot with butter.

Cover the filling with the second pie crust circle (for top crust). Lift bottom crust slightly and fold top crust under. Crimp edges of crust. Cut slits in top crust to let steam escape.

Lightly brush top of pie with milk and sprinkle with sugar.

To prevent over-browning, cover the edge of pie crust with edge protectors or foil. Bake for 40 minutes; then remove edge protectors or foil. Bake for an additional 20 minutes, or until fruit is tender and filling is bubbly. Tip: If top crust browns too quickly, cover loosely with foil.

Cool on wire rack. To serve warm, let pie cool at least 2 hours.

I am a single parent of two boys.

So to spend time with them that is not too girlish, I would find things that would be fun for them. We made this together every year until they grew up.

The first time we made this was on the Fourth of July. Everyone thought the boys were being helpful by decorating the table with a pot of artificial flowers.

The reaction on their faces when they would pinch some of the "dirt" to eat... **it still makes me smile today thinking about it.**

Every year they have "gotten" someone, thinking they were eating dirt. **This is something I will always cherish.** The memories of my boys when they tricked people will never be forgotten.

TAMMY HELZER

POT O' DIRT

INGREDIENTS

1 large package Oreo cookies

4 tablespoons butter

1 - 8 ounce package cream cheese

1 cup powdered sugar

3 ½ cups milk

2 packages instant French vanilla pudding

1 - 12 ounce carton Cool Whip

8 inch diameter (at top) new clay pot or plastic pot

Artificial flowers to insert into dessert

3 to 4 gummi worms (optional)

INSTRUCTIONS

Crush well one whole package of Oreo cookies. Set aside. Cream together butter, cream cheese and powered sugar. In separate bowl, mix together milk and pudding mix, add to creamed mixture. Fold in Cool Whip.

Plug hole in pot by placing a plastic container lid into bottom of pot.

Layer cookies and pudding mixture. End with cookies. Refrigerate. (Recipe should be cut in half for smaller pot.)

Decorate with worms going up and down on top and add flowers before serving.

PEOPLE SERVED: 12

DESSERTS

The first time I had these cookies was at a family reunion. My cousin made them and they were so good I got the recipe from her.

After reading the recipe I realized this was a HUGE mix.

After going out and buying the biggest mixing bowl I could find I spent the next 5-6 hours making them,

whew!!!

JEANNIE HARRISON

MONSTER COOKIES

INGREDIENTS

12 eggs

2 pounds brown sugar

4 cups white sugar

1 tablespoon white syrup

1 tablespoon vanilla extract

8 teaspoons baking soda

1 pound peanut butter

18 cups of Snoqualmie Falls oatmeal *(quick oats work best)*

1 pound of candy coated chocolates

1 pound of chocolate chips

INSTRUCTIONS

Cream the butter with the brown and white sugar.

Add eggs, syrup, vanilla, and baking soda. Add the peanut butter.

Hand mix the oatmeal, candy and chocolate chips.

Bake at 350°F. for 8-10 minutes. I use 3 pieces of parchment paper to bake them: one in the oven baking, one cooling and one ready to go in the oven.

Great cookies to freeze for later.

PEOPLE SERVED: 1 FAMILY REUNION

DESSERTS

"Waste not, Want not" is one of the many principles that my dear mother Dorie has instilled in all of us growing up.

She did not call it "recycling" then, the way we commonly use the term now, whether re-using containers, re-purposing items, or saving leftover food to be used somehow with another recipe, or giving it another interesting name.

The blueberry bread pudding recipe came out of my desire not to waste the leftover samples of Krusteaz crumb cake that the R&D lab has no need for after the sensory evaluation was completed.

The crusty cake pieces that was a result of being on the sides of the pan was the perfect initial ingredient for my first blueberry pudding bake test.

No part of the baked cake was thrown away, not a crumb...

ALITHA EDWARDS

BLUEBERRY BREAD PUDDING

INGREDIENTS

6 cups Krusteaz crumb cake, cubed

4 tablespoons butter, melted

2 cups milk

4 eggs

1 teaspoon vanilla extract

1 cup fresh blueberries (frozen blueberries can be substituted)

PEOPLE SERVED: 12 TO 15

INSTRUCTIONS

Preheat standard oven to 350°F.

Fill a lightly greased 13x9x2-inch metal pan with the crumb cake.

In a separate bowl, mix together eggs, milk and vanilla extract. Then pour mixed liquid ingredients over the cubed crumb cake.

Top with blueberries. Drizzle with melted butter for a final touch prior to baking.

Bake for 25 to 30 minutes at 350°F. oven.

Let rest for at least 15 minutes before serving. Can be served hot or cold.

Optional:

½ cup of nuts can be added to the recipe if so desired, along with 1 to 2 tablespoons of your favorite liqueur. Great for special occasions. Adjust baking time accordingly.

Pfeffernuesse or "pepper nuts" are a traditional German Christmas cookie.

Every year during the holidays, my family could count on a big batch of these crunchy, spiced little morsels placed in bowls and jars throughout my grandma Caroline's home for all to enjoy.

My mom tells stories about how growing up, she would be so nervous making sure each little cookie was cut to the same size that she would often use a ruler to measure.

These days, I attempt to make perfectly uniform, tasty little pepper nuts in **memory of my grandma.**

Not sure they'll ever be as good as hers, but **she'd certainly be proud to be sharing this recipe with you!**

JENNIFER SMITH

GRANDMA CAROLINE'S PFEFFERNUESSE

INGREDIENTS

8 cups all-purpose flour

1 cup shortening

1 cup butter

2 cups sugar

1 cup molasses

3 eggs

½ cup sour milk
(teaspoon lemon juice/distilled vinegar added to milk)

½ teaspoon anise oil

1 teaspoon cinnamon

½ teaspoon black pepper

½ teaspoon ground cardamom

1 teaspoon salt

1 teaspoon baking soda

1 teaspoon cloves

½ teaspoon walnut flavor (optional)

INSTRUCTIONS

Preheat oven to 350°F.

Mix all ingredients together until well blended.

Wrap dough in saran wrap and chill in freezer overnight, keeping dough as cold as possible. While still frozen, slice and portion out dough and roll into several 12-18 inch long ropes (diameter of a pinky finger). Cut into ½ - ¾ inch pieces (should look like little pillows).

Place in rows on baking sheet and bake for 7-9 minutes.

Cool. Remove from sheet and enjoy!

PEOPLE SERVED: GOBS!

DESSERTS

Grandma Rosemarie is wonderful in the kitchen and this recipe was one that she began making for family birthdays and celebrations. This moist and delicious chocolate cake is complemented with a smooth and creamy peanut butter frosting.

It has been a traditional family favorite for many years.

Grandma's dad began calling her 'Cookie' when she was a little girl and the name stuck.

The recipe eventually became 'Cookie Grammy's Famous Chocolate Cake with Peanut Butter Frosting' and the rest they say, is history.

I hope your family enjoys it as much as we do!

GREG SEVENER

COOKIE GRAMMY'S FAMOUS CHOCOLATE CAKE WITH PEANUT BUTTER FROSTING

INGREDIENTS

Cake:

2 cups sugar

2 cups flour

¾ cup cocoa

1 teaspoon baking powder

2 teaspoons baking soda

1 teaspoon salt

½ cup vegetable oil

1 cup coffee, brewed

1 cup milk

2 eggs

2 teaspoons vanilla

Peanut Butter Frosting:

1 cup milk

3 tablespoons flour

½ cup butter

½ cup peanut butter, smooth

1 cup sugar

1 teaspoon vanilla

INSTRUCTIONS

Cake:

Combine dry ingredients in a bowl. Add all other ingredients and beat for 4 minutes. Lightly grease and flour a 9x13-inch pan and bake at 350°F. for 35-45 minutes.

Peanut Butter Frosting:

Combine flour and milk to a smooth paste. Cook in heat safe bowl over boiling water, stirring frequently until mixture is thick like custard - 4 to 5 minutes. Remove from heat and cover immediately to prevent a top film from forming. Set aside to cool.

Cream butter, peanut butter, sugar and vanilla well. Combine creamed mixture with custard, beating until good spreading consistency.

ADDITIONAL NOTES

You can also use two 8 or 9-inch round pans or a lined cupcake pan.

PEOPLE SERVED: 6-8

DESSERTS

This Chocolate Mousse was my mom's personal creation and was **ultimately my inspiration for going into cooking professionally.**

I did embellish the recipe slightly into its present form.

DIMITRI PONOMARCHUK

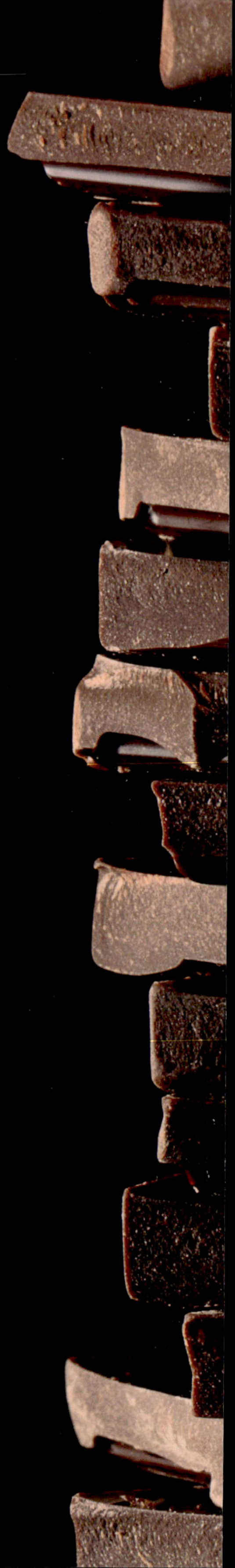

CHOCOLATE MOUSSE

INGREDIENTS

18 ounces semi-sweet chocolate

2 cups heavy cream, chilled

6 eggs, separated

2 tablespoons granulated sugar

2 tablespoons dark rum

1 tablespoon vanilla extract

INSTRUCTIONS

Melt chocolate in a double boiler. Cool until warm.

Whip cream until soft peaks are formed. Beat the egg yolks until light and creamy. Whip the egg whites with sugar until soft peaks are formed.

Combine the chocolate and the beaten egg yolks, mixing over warm water. When completely incorporated, add some of the whipped cream and incorporate gently. Add the remaining cream.

Repeat the same procedure with the whipped egg whites. Blend in the rum. Do not over beat.

PEOPLE SERVED: 6-8

DESSERTS

Mom was a great cook and her banana pudding was her signature dish.

In 1954, my parents took a leap of faith and moved from rural Alabama to Southern California for better opportunity for their children. During my youth many family members from Alabama made a similar trek and most ended up living with us for some period of time while they settled into the big city.

Sunday dinner at our house was the event that gathered those relatives living in LA and those recently arrived.

My mom's banana pudding **symbolizes the sacrifices** made by my parents and extended family for better opportunities for their children and generations that followed.

Enjoy!

CLYDE WALKER

BEULAH MAE'S OLD FASHIONED BANANA PUDDING

INGREDIENTS

Pudding Ingredients:

1 cup sugar

½ cup all-purpose flour

½ teaspoon salt

2 cups milk (NOT skim)

4 or 5 ripe bananas, sliced thin
(cover with plastic wrap or sprinkle with lemon juice to keep them from turning brown)

1 box vanilla wafers

1 teaspoon vanilla extract

1 tablespoon butter (not margarine)

4 egg yolks (large eggs or better)

Meringue ingredients:

4 egg whites, room temperature

5 tablespoons sugar

¼ teaspoon cream of tartar

½ teaspoon vanilla extract

PEOPLE SERVED: A LOT

INSTRUCTIONS

Preheat oven to 375°F.

Line the bottom of a 9x9-inch pan with a layer of vanilla wafers.

Combine sugar, flour and salt in a bowl, and mix well. Set aside.

In a heavy saucepan, beat the egg yolks well.

Over medium heat, add the flour mixture to the egg yolks, alternately with the milk and vanilla, stirring constantly. Bring to a gentle boil and, when the mixture begins to thicken, add the butter, continuing to stir. Keep boiling and stirring until mixture reaches a nice pudding consistency. Make sure you don't scorch the pudding. Remove from heat.

Place a layer of banana slices on top of the vanilla wafers. Pour half of the pudding over the banana layer. Put down another layer of vanilla wafers, another layer of banana slices, and cover with the remaining pudding.

Beat the egg whites at high speed until they form soft peaks. Add the cream of tartar. At high speed, gradually add the sugar, a tablespoon at a time, and beat until stiff peaks form. Fold the vanilla into the meringue, and spread the meringue over the pudding, sealing it at the sides of the dish.

Bake until meringue browns, 12 to 15 minutes.

DESSERTS

The first time I had this pie it was made for me by my boyfriend who was trying to impress me with his baking skills.

It took about 2 years and many pies before he confessed to me how simple it was to make.

I've brought this pie to many pot-lucks and it always gets wonderful reviews.

I've even been told by true pecan pie lovers that it's one of, if not the best pecan pie, they've ever had!

TIFFANY LUBY

SOUTHERN PECAN PIE

INGREDIENTS

1 cup light corn syrup

3 eggs

1 cup sugar (brown or white)

2 tablespoons butter melted

1 teaspoon pure vanilla extract

1 ½ cups pecans

1 - 9-inch unbaked or prepared pie crust

ADDITIONAL NOTES

If you use white sugar instead of brown or light brown sugar the taste will be a little less sweet.

INSTRUCTIONS

Preheat oven to 350°F.

Mix corn syrup, eggs, sugar, butter and vanilla with a spoon.

Stir in pecans.

Pour filling into pie crust.

Bake on center rack of oven for 60 to 70 minutes.

Cool before serving.

Spray pie plate with cooking spray before place pie crust in plate for easier serving and clean-up. If crust is overbrowning, cover edges with aluminum foil.

PEOPLE SERVED: 8

DESSERTS

This was my great-grandmother's recipe. I had gotten from my granny. **She always made a fruit cake every year for Christmas; the old fashioned kind just after Thanksgiving.**

She would put it in the lard stand wrapped in cloth to soak in some kind of whiskey or brandy to keep it moist.

It was **a favorite of my dad's,** and he always took enough home with him to last until next Christmas.

My Little Mama was a great woman-she lived to be 98 years old.

She was like a Mama to me.

LISA BIRD

LITTLE MAMA'S FRUIT CAKE RECIPE

INGREDIENTS

- 1 small can candied cherries
- 1 small can pineapples
- 8 ounce box dates
- 15 ounce box raisins
- 2 ¾ ounces walnuts
- 2 ¾ ounces pecans (save ½ of the package for icing
- 1 cup flour, all-purpose
- 3 ½ ounce can coconut
- 1 cup of Crisco
- 4 eggs
- 1 cup sugar
- ½ cup brown sugar
- 1 teaspoon cinnamon
- 1 teaspoon nutmeg
- 1 teaspoon allspice
- 1 teaspoon coffee (short teaspoon)
- 1 heaping tablespoon cocoa
- 5 ounces strawberry preserves
- ⅓ cup honey
- ⅓ cup whiskey
- 1 teaspoon vanilla
- ½ cup buttermilk
- 1 teaspoon baking powder
- 1 teaspoon salt (sprinkle over batter)
- 1 heaping teaspoon baking soda (mix this and baking powder in the buttermilk)
- 1 cup water

INSTRUCTIONS

Save all juice from candied fruit for the cake batter.

Mix cherries, pineapple, ⅔ cup dates, ⅓ cup raisins, 2 ¾ ounces of walnuts, 1 cup flour, coconut and 2 ¾ of pecans (mix well).

Cream the white and brown sugar with Crisco. Mix the reserved juice with the soda and buttermilk.

Mix eggs, cinnamon, nutmeg, allspice, coffee, cocoa, strawberry preserves honey, whiskey, vanilla, salt and baking powder that was mixed with juice soda and buttermilk previously. (mix well)

Grease and flour two loaf pans. Put half of the batter in each pan. Bake at 300ºF. for one hour.

Icing

- 1 cup brown sugar
- 1 cup white sugar
- ½ cup raisins (heaping)
- ⅓ box dates
- 1 cup of water

Add remaining pecans.

Cook until ready. Add coconut.

Cool and add walnuts. Save a little fruit and nuts to decorate top.

Get two pieces of cardboard, cut to the size of the cakes, wrap cardboard with aluminum foil. Place cakes on aluminum wrapped cardboards. Sprinkle each layer with whiskey, ice cakes. Place a piece of cheesecloth on top of each cake that is big enough to cover the top of each cake. Sprinkle cheesecloth topped cake with remaining whiskey.

Place cakes in airtight containers. Keep cloth moistened with additional whiskey if needed.

PEOPLE SERVED: 12 - 14

DESSERTS

The **Puderbaugh family** always got together for Christmas Eve at **Grandma and Grandpa's house**. Grandma always made her special Peanut Butter Fudge during the holidays and it was like no other fudge I have ever tasted, melting in your mouth instantly.

It was also Aunt Margie's birthday so there was always a store bought Christmas decorated sheet cake for her birthday. Before opening gifts, Grandpa always read the Christmas Story from the Bible. We then opened gifts and celebrated Aunt Margie's birthday with cake and **Grandma's homemade fudge** for dessert.

For Christmas, **Grandma always made things** for the girls in the family i.e. aprons, knitted scarves, etc., the guys received a pair of socks, and there was a small toy for each child. **Those were simple times when gifts were made from Grandma's bare hands** and the fudge she made from scratch was like the *icing on the cake!*

SHELLEY VANDERPOEL

GRANDMA PUDERBAUGH'S PEANUT BUTTER FUDGE

INGREDIENTS

2 cups white sugar

2 tablespoons butter

1 tablespoon peanut butter

½ cup milk

1 tablespoon vanilla

⅓ cup peanuts (no skins)

1 - 7 ounce jar marshmallow cream

INSTRUCTIONS

Combine sugar, butter and milk in heavy pan. Bring to a full rolling boil, stirring constantly. Continue boiling for 5 minutes over medium heat.

Remove from heat; add peanut butter until blended; then add marshmallow cream, nuts and vanilla.

Beat until well blended. Pour onto lightly greased cookie sheet.

Cool at room temperature and then cut into bite size pieces and enjoy!

This recipe is as simple as the times were back then.

ADDITIONAL NOTES

I use a 10 ½ x15-inch cookie pan, but it makes fairly shallow fudge. Use a pan or baking sheet you don't mind cutting on as it will leave knife marks. You

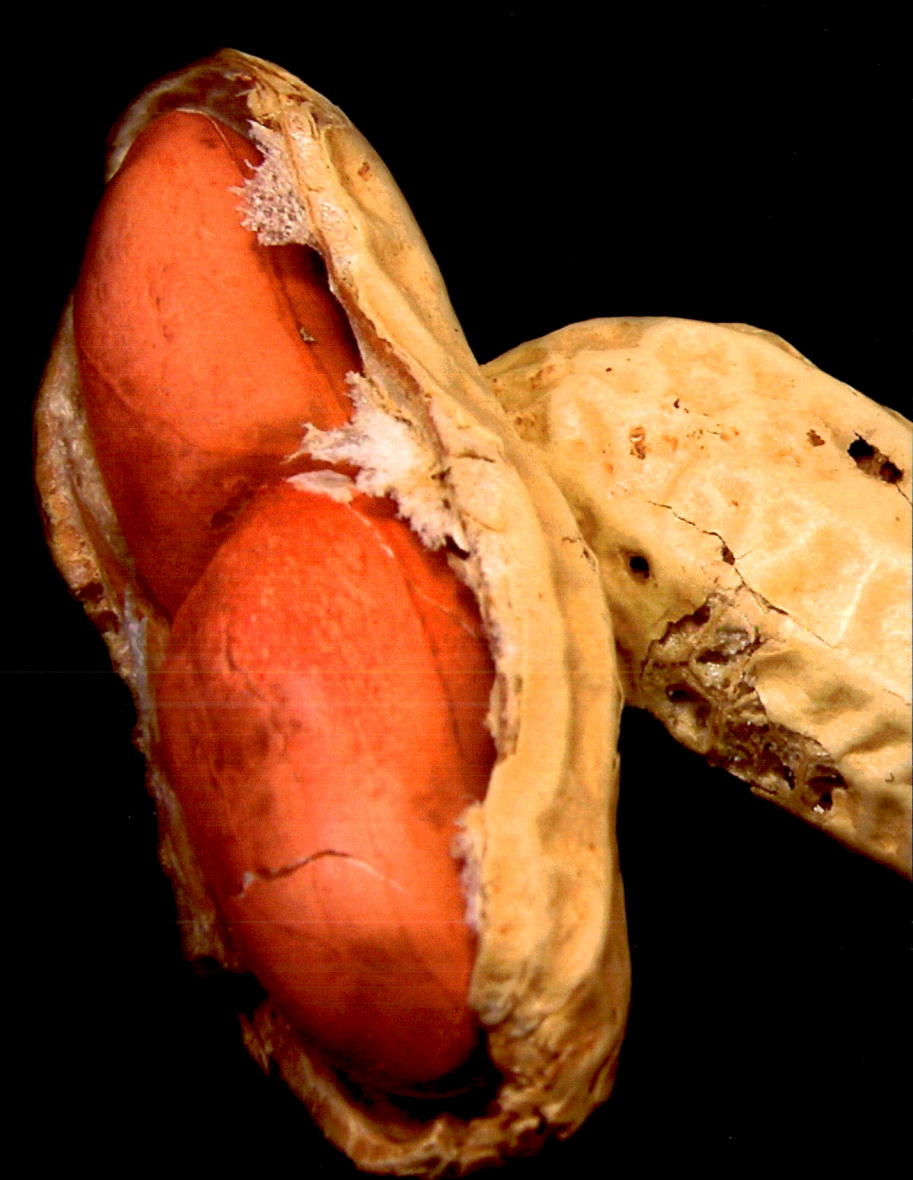

DESSERTS

Early in our marriage, we were introduced to Eli's cheesecake. It was boxed and sold in grocery stores. We loved it but it was expensive. Linda decided to make a cheesecake at home to have a special treat and save money.

She made a cheesecake and brought me a piece as proud as could be. I tried a bite and when asked how it was, I replied **"It's not ready to be boxed up yet."**

About 15 years later, she surprised me with another cheesecake. This one was really good (*I may be biased*). I put it on the list for Christmas and it has been a hit. She makes several different kinds of cheesecake but they are now being boxed up and given away as Christmas gifts.

I love that my wife stuck with it and now has developed something **that we can share with the people I work with.**

MIKE CHURCHILL

LINDA'S CHEESECAKE

INGREDIENTS

Crust

4 ½ cups crushed Oreo cookies

1 cup chopped roasted peanuts

½ cup butter, melted

Filling

2 pounds cream cheese, softened

5 eggs, at room temperature

1 ½ cups firmly packed brown sugar

1 cup smooth peanut butter (not natural-style)

½ cup whipping cream

1 teaspoon vanilla extract

12 Reese's peanut butter cups, broken into small pieces

Topping

5 ounces milk chocolate chips and ⅓ cup sour cream

INSTRUCTIONS

Please Note:

Plan ahead - cheesecake needs to chill for at least 4 hours.

To Make The Crust:

Combine crushed Oreo cookies and peanuts that have been ground in a food processor with the melted butter.

Pat the crust mixture onto bottom and sides of a 10-inch spring form pan.

To Make The Filling:

Beat cream cheese in bowl of electric mixer until smooth.

Add eggs, one at a time, beating well after each addition.

Add sugar, peanut butter and cream; mix until smooth.

Stir in vanilla, then fold in peanut butter cup pieces with a rubber spatula. Pour filling into prepared crust.

Bake at 450°F. for 15 minutes then reduce oven temperature to 200°F. Bake for two hours, then turn off the oven and leave the cheesecake in for another two hours. This slow cooling will help prevent cracking.

Remove the cheesecake from the oven and allow to cool to room temperature. You may run a knife along the edge of the cake to loosen it from the pan somewhat.

Melt 5 ounces of chocolate chips in the microwave (30 seconds at half power then stir, repeating this process until melted. Be careful, it can burn if you cook it too long!). Stir in ⅓ cup sour cream, mix well and pour over top of cheesecake. Chill in refrigerator for at least 4 hours before serving!

PEOPLE SERVED: 10

DESSERTS

When my **mom** was a new bride, she learned to make this recipe from a neighbor friend who spent time showing her how to make this recipe.

It's been a family favorite recipe ever since!

ROSEMARY SMALBERG

DANISH ALMOND PUFF

INGREDIENTS

Pastry:

½ cup butter, cut in pieces

1 cup flour

4-5 tablespoons cold water

Almond Topping:

1 cup water

½ cup butter

1 teaspoon almond extract

1 cup flour

3 eggs

Powdered sugar glaze

Almonds, chopped or slivered

INSTRUCTIONS

Preheat oven to 350°F.

To make the pastry, place flour in mixing bowl. Using a fork or pastry blender, cut in ½ cup butter until mixture is crumbly. Add water, 1 tablespoon at a time until mixture forms a dough.

Divide the dough in half and place on an ungreased baking sheet. Pat out dough 3 inches apart into 2 strips each about 12x3 inches. Set aside.

To make almond topping, place water and ½ cup butter in a medium saucepan and bring ring to a boil. Remove sauce pan from heat and stir in almond extract. Add flour and stir until mixture is smooth. Using an electric mixer, add eggs one at a time and blend until mixture pulls away from the sides of the pan.

Spoon mixture equally onto 2 strips of dough in baking pan; spread to smooth evenly. Bake 1 hour or until top is golden brown and puffy.

Cool completely; then drizzle with powdered sugar glaze. Sprinkle with chopped or slivered almonds.

Enjoy!

PEOPLE SERVED: 12

DESSERTS

WONDERFUL LEMON CAKE

INGREDIENTS

1 package lemon or yellow cake mix

1 package lemon Jell-O

¾ cup water

4 eggs

¾ cup vegetable oil

2 cups powdered sugar

⅔ cups lemon juice

PEOPLE SERVED: 12 SERVINGS

INSTRUCTIONS

Beat together 1 package cake mix, 1 package lemon Jell-O, ¾ cup water, and 4 eggs.

Beat about 3 minutes on medium speed. Add ¾ cup vegetable oil and beat another minute or two, until well blended.

Pour into a 9X13-inch aluminum baking pan and bake according to the boxed cake mix directions. When done, remove from oven and poke with a fork so that the cake is full of holes.

Make up 2 cups of powdered sugar with ⅔ cups of lemon juice and mix together. (Mixture should be fairly thin, if not add more lemon juice.

Pour over cake and serve with cool whip or other whipped topping.

My grandmother used to make really yummy desserts back in the 50's and my brother and I would always look forward to this Lemon Cake.

WENDY FRANZ

DESSERTS

This recipe came from my daughter's teacher. Their class project was to shop for ingredients and bake cookies to sell to other students.

After they made them she brought some home for MOM and I LOVED THEM!!

SOFT CHOCOLATE CHIP COOKIES

INGREDIENTS

4 ½ cups flour

2 teaspoons baking soda

2 cups butter, softened

1 ½ cups packed brown sugar

½ cup white sugar

2 small packages instant vanilla pudding mix

4 eggs

3 teaspoons vanilla extract

2 cups chocolate chips

INSTRUCTIONS

Preheat oven to 350°F.

Sift together the flour and baking soda, set aside.

In a large bowl, cream together the butter, brown sugar and white sugar. Beat in the instant pudding mix until blended. Stir in the eggs and vanilla. Blend in the flour mixture.

FINALLY, stir in the chocolate chips.

Drop cookies by rounded spoonfuls onto a greased cookie sheet.

Bake for 10 to 12 minutes in a preheated oven.

PEOPLE SERVED: 8

DESSERTS

I was very close to my grandmother, Lola Jack.

I lived with her when I was very young and spent summers at my grandparents when I was growing up. She taught me to knit, crochet, cook and bake.

One day we were looking through a box of old pictures and memories and came across a ration booklet with stamps from when my grandfather was in WWII. She explained during the wars people were limited in what they could purchase and had to come up with ways of using less staples like flour and sugar.

Cake was really a luxury item.

Her mother-in-law, great grandma Vi, grew up during the depression and had family that fought in WWI. She was a VERY frugal woman and was always making everything stretch.

The aroma of this rich spice cake makes me feel like I'm right back in my grandma's kitchen.

TAMI BURKLEY

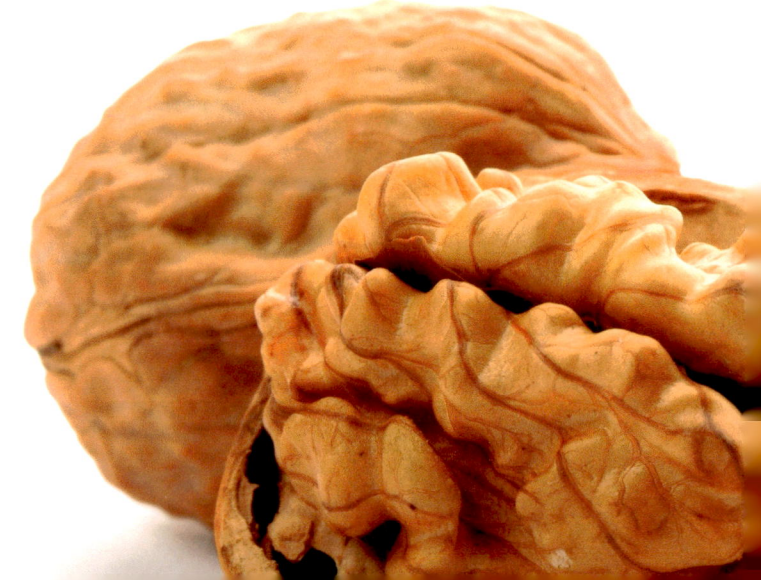

GREAT GRANDMA VI'S WORLD WAR I CAKE

INGREDIENTS

2 ¼ cups all-purpose flour

1 ¼ cups granulated sugar

1 tablespoon corn starch

¼ teaspoon ground nutmeg

¼ teaspoon ground cloves

1 teaspoon ground cinnamon

½ teaspoon salt

1 ½ cups chunky applesauce

2 cups raisins

½ cups vegetable shortening

1 egg

1 cup chopped walnuts

1 teaspoon baking soda

Cooking spray

INSTRUCTIONS

Preheat oven to 325°F.

Lightly spray bundt pan with cooking spray. Sift first 7 dry ingredients together 3 times into a large mixing bowl

Place raisins in medium sauce pan and add water just to cover. Over medium high heat bring raisins to a boil for 3 to 5 minutes until they plump up. Remove from heat, strain water from raisins and add vegetable shortening, stir until melted.

Add applesauce, raisins and egg to dry ingredients. Stir until smooth and the dry ingredients are incorporated. Mix in walnuts.

Dissolve the baking soda into a tablespoon of hot water and stir into batter. Pour batter into bundt pan using a spatula to smooth the top. Batter will be thick.

Bake 1 hour, then test for doneness with a toothpick.

PEOPLE SERVED: 8-12

DESSERTS

Every Christmas, my great grandma Pete always made Norwegian Krumkake.

As a child, I have vivid memories of tin cans filled with these delicate cone shaped cookies. She would also make many, many cookies to give away as gifts.

Grandma came to the states from Norway in 1910 at the age of 10 and brought with her this Norwegian tradition. It has been **passed down the generations and continues as a family tradition today.**

This last Christmas, my mom and I enjoyed spending an afternoon together making these treats to give as gifts.

Although our family enjoys these crispy cookie cones "naked", they are also fun to fill with flavored whip cream.

LEIGH ANN STEBENS

NORWEGIAN KRUMKAKE

INGREDIENTS

1 cup sugar

½ cup unsalted butter, melted and cooled slightly

2 large eggs

½ cup heavy whipping cream

½ cup milk

1 ½ cups all-purpose flour

¾ teaspoon cardamom

1 teaspoon vanilla

½ teaspoon salt

INSTRUCTIONS

In a medium bowl, cream 1 cup sugar with melted butter until combined. Add eggs and beat for 2 minutes or until the mixture has turned light yellow in color. Add milk, cream, flour, vanilla, cardamom and salt and blend until smooth. Let stand 30 minutes.

Preheat a cast iron krumkake iron on stove (as my grandma did) or use an electric krumkake maker*. Spray iron lightly with nonstick spray.

Spoon 1-2 tablespoons of the batter onto center of the hot iron. Bake for about 1 – 1 ½ minutes, or until cookie is light brown.

Carefully remove from iron and quickly (short window of time for molding) roll the hot cookie into a cone shape using a cone mold*.

Once out of the maker, there is a short amount of time to mold before the cookies get crisp. Repeat with remaining batter.

If batter thickens, add a little water as necessary to thin the consistency.

Store the baked cookies in an airtight container for up to 2 weeks.

*available at kitchen stores

PEOPLE SERVED: ABOUT 2 DOZEN CONES

DESSERTS

STRAWBERRY DANISH DELIGHT

INGREDIENTS

1 angel food cake

1 block cream cheese

1 tub Cool Whip

INSTRUCTIONS

Tear your angel food cake into small pieces and place in a cake pan.

Sit cream cheese out to soften then add cool whip and blend together with mixer add your

ETCETERA!

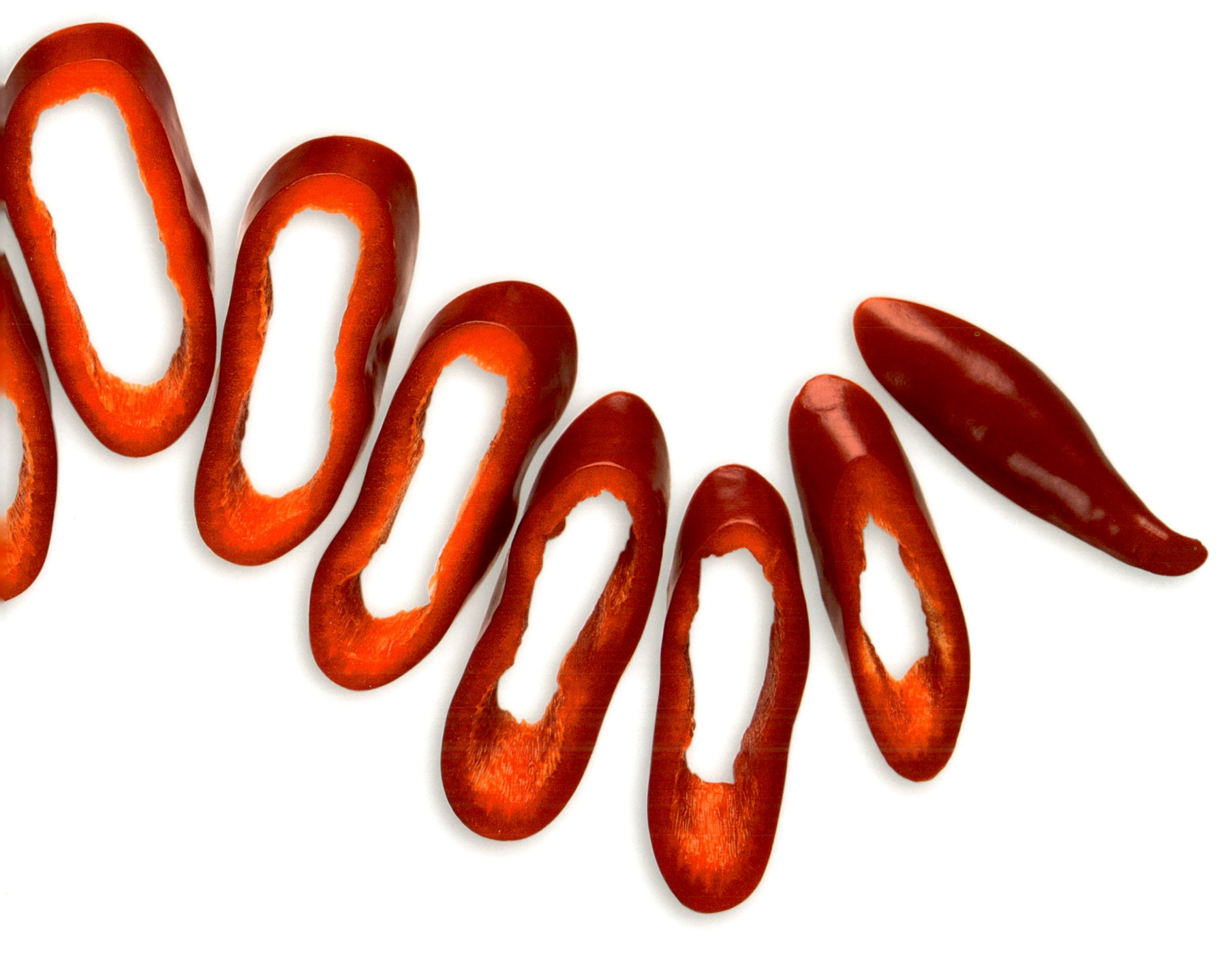

Many years ago, I was fooling around in the kitchen trying to come up with a sauce that was similar to the hot mustard on barbecued pork served at Chinese restaurants. I put together my **"Secret Sauce"** - which is a hot and spicy sauce to be served with pork or salmon.

My favorite story about my **super-duper extra-special Secret Sauce** was one occasion when my wife, Deeanna, was having six of her friends over for a special dinner which she worked all day putting together. I left for the evening only to arrive home after her friends had left, to hear **the hit of her dinner was my Secret Sauce.**

JOHN HEILY

JOHNNY'S SECRET SAUCE

INGREDIENTS

½ cup mayonnaise

1 heaping tablespoon Colman's Mustard (dry)

1 tablespoon dijon mustard (preferably Grey Poupon)

1 tablespoon prepared horseradish

INSTRUCTIONS

The secret of my *Secret Sauce* is Colman's Dry mustard and the directions are as follows:

Mix the Colman's mustard with a small amount of warm water (about 1 heaping tablespoon) to form a slurry.

Mix together the rest of the ingredients and add the Colman's mustard slurry. Mix well.

It is important for the *Secret Sauce* to sit for at least 30 minutes to develop the flavor. The heat in this sauce mellows as it rests. It is a bit of an understatement to say, but "adjust to taste"!

PEOPLE SERVED: 4

ETCETERA

I came across this in an online search for recipes and just had to try it out. I put my sauce into mini pint jars, labeled them and gave them out for Christmas presents around work this last year.

What a huge hit that was!

It was so good over ice cream and even better just eating it as it cooled down enough not to burn the tongue.

It won't last long if you have chocolate lovers at your house.

SANDRA BENSLEY

HOT FUDGE SAUCE

INGREDIENTS

1 cube (stick, ½ cup) butter, soft

1 cup chocolate chips

1 can sweetened condensed milk

INSTRUCTIONS

In a medium sauce pan on medium heat, melt the butter. Stir in the chocolate chips. Add the sweetened condensed milk.

Stir well to combine. The butter will take a minute to incorporate into the sauce. It will be smooth and silky.

Store any leftovers in the refrigerator.

Good for one month in sealed container.

PEOPLE SERVED: MAKES SEVERAL PINT JARS

ETCETERA

DOUGHNUTS

INGREDIENTS

1 cup sugar

2 eggs beaten

¼ teaspoon lemon extract

3 tablespoons melted shortening

4 cups flour

4 teaspoons baking powder

½ teaspoon salt

½ teaspoon nutmeg

1 cup milk

INSTRUCTIONS

Add sugar gradually to eggs, beating thoroughly. Add extract and shortening.

Slowly add sifted dry ingredients and milk, mix well after each addition. Knead lightly on a lightly floured counter.

Roll out ½ inch thick and cut with a doughnut cutter. Drop into oil heated to 350°F. and fry until golden brown, turning once.

Drain on paper towel. Roll in sugar or powdered sugar while warm.

PEOPLE SERVED: 4

This is an old family recipe handed down from my mother-in-law.

She made them every Christmas Eve for 40 years!

Now I do it, if the family doesn't see homemade doughnuts on Christmas Eve and leftovers for Christmas morning, it just isn't Christmas.

DONNA AKIN

ETCETERA

A family favorite for Christmas morning, this recipe came from a long ago holiday magazine.

The cut out piece of paper is now very wrinkled and fragile, somehow surviving in the old recipe box, but the photo of the finished bread is still colorful.

I was happy to find my grown children still making this yummy bread and carrying on the tradition.

BOBBI MILLER

TWISTREE BREAD

INGREDIENTS

2 ¾ to 3 cups all-purpose flour, sifted

1 envelope active dry yeast

¼ teaspoon baking soda

1 teaspoon salt

1 cup buttermilk

¼ cup shortening

¼ cup sugar

1 egg

2 tablespoons butter or margarine, softened

Red and green sugar crystals

PEOPLE SERVED: 8 - 10

INSTRUCTIONS

Preheat oven to 375°F.

Combine 1 ½ cups flour, yeast, and baking soda.

Heat buttermilk, shortening, sugar, and salt until warm, stirring to melt shortening.

Add to dry ingredients, add egg. Beat at low speed ½ minute, scraping bowl constantly. Beat 3 minutes at high speed. Stir in enough remaining flour to make moderately stiff.

Turn onto floured board, knead 5 minutes. Cover with cloth, let rest 10 minutes. Halve dough. Roll one half to 14x6-inch rectangle.

Spread with 1 tablespoon butter or margarine; sprinkle with 1 tablespoon red sugar crystals. Fold in half to make narrow rectangle. Cut into fourteen 1-inch strips.

Twist each one and arrange on greased baking sheet in tree shape. Repeat with remaining dough, butter, and 1 tablespoon green sugar crystals.

Let rise 1 hour.

Bake in 375°F. oven for 15 minutes, let cool.

Frost with confectioners' icing, if desired.

ETCETERA

For something so simple, these are absolutely to die for. I can eat a half pan of them all by myself. This recipe is from my **grandfather** who was a baker and knew what he was doing.

Both my grandfather and my grandmother were good cooks, but **he won my top prize for these popovers.**

Everyone who eats these treats loves them and requests the recipe, so I am providing it now for everyone.

KATHY FREED

GRANDAD'S BEST POPOVERS

INGREDIENTS

2 cups flour

1 teaspoon salt

2 cups milk

4 large eggs

PEOPLE SERVED: 2-8

INSTRUCTIONS

Preheat oven to 425°F.

Beat all ingredients together on low speed with a mixer until smooth, 1-2 minutes.

Spray a muffin tin with non-stick spray. Fill each muffin cup about ⅔ full with batter.

Bake at 425°F. for about 30 minutes or until well browned.

Let cool only until you can touch them without getting burned. Pull apart and slather with butter or jam.

These are best when eaten hot. They do not store well.

ETCETERA

One of my fond memories of my Grandma Spatz was her teaching me how to make Sunday dinner rolls. I must have been around **7 or 8 years old at the time** and took to it with enthusiasm. Before long, I became the designated dinner roll baker -

Grandma turned the tradition over to me!

As the years progressed, I made all kinds of yeast breads. The last half of my 9 years in 4-H, I took the Foods project and concentrated on yeast breads. In a white bread loaf competition, **I won 2nd place** out of 24 participants.

The following year I won **Reserved Champion** in the Open competition for a beautiful cinnamon roll coffee cake. An elderly lady was quite appalled by **the fact a teenager beat her at this event!** I did not need the ribbon to be proud of my achievement after hearing her fuss! All of this was done using a recipe handed out to kids in 4-H.

That was back 35 years ago and this submitted recipe is an improved version of it used at our holiday meals to create the **yeast rolls and cinnamon rolls that make each holiday even brighter.**

MARK DAVIDSON

BETTER THAN GRANDMA'S YEAST ROLLS

INGREDIENTS

6 cups all purpose flour

2 packages active dry yeast

½ cup sugar

1 tablespoon salt

2 eggs (beaten)

2 cups 2% milk (warm)

½ cup Crisco shortening

PEOPLE SERVED: 24 YEAST ROLLS

INSTRUCTIONS

Preheat oven to 375°F.

Add 3 cups flour and dry yeast together in a large bowl and blend thoroughly.

Add sugar, eggs, salt and warm milk (less than 110°F). Mix with your favorite wooden spoon until a smooth batter is formed. While stirring, begin adding additional cups of flour until a stiff dough forms.

Turn dough out onto a well floured cutting board and begin kneading for about 10 minutes or until the dough is velvety and smooth.

Place dough in large, greased bowl, cover with plastic wrap or a tea towel. Allow the dough to double in size (ferment) in a warm place.

"Punch" the dough to release the gas produced by the yeast fermenting. Divide dough into 24 equal sized pieces. Stretch the skin of the dough pieces to create smooth uniform balls.

Evenly space rolls in a 9x13-inch greased pan in a 4x6 configuration. Lightly cover with a tea towel and place in warm area until rolls have doubled.

Bake rolls at 375°F. for 20 - 25 minutes or until rolls are golden brown and sound hollow when tapped with a finger. Immediately brush with melted butter before serving.

This same dough can be used to create cinnamon rolls or coffee cakes.

Yum Yum!!!

My grama made the best graham bread, I have never tasted or even seen anything like it anywhere else.

On the farm, they would eat the large meal at noon, then the evenings would be more like lunch with open faced sandwiches made with grama's homemade graham bread.

I would always be right there in that huge country kitchen ready to eat the first piece she would cut, still hot from the oven and smothered in butter.

Maybe grama had a secret that was never written down. We will never know but mom has done a pretty good job recreating this yummy bread.

CATHIE BUNCH

GRAMA'S OLD FASHIONED GRAHAM BREAD

INGREDIENTS

2 cups warm water

1 package yeast

2 teaspoons salt

2 tablespoons sugar

2 tablespoons oil

1 tablespoon molasses

4 cups graham flour or stone ground whole wheat flour

INSTRUCTIONS

Preheat oven to 350°F.

Mix all ingredients together, knead well.

Shape into 2 small-medium loaf pans (smaller than usual bread pans).

Let rise for about 10 minutes.

Bake for 30 minutes at 350°F. then another 30 minutes at 325°F.

PEOPLE SERVED: 10 OR MORE

ETCETERA

These yummy breakfast bars are high in protein and antioxidants and have no grain or sugar. They are naturally sweet from the fruits and are a terrific gluten-free option.

SHEILA JIRKA

BREAKFAST BARS

INGREDIENTS

8 eggs

4 cups almond meal

2 cups cooked and chopped sweet potatoes

2 cups mashed ripe bananas

8-10 chopped Medjool dates (discard the pits!)

½ cup unsweetened shredded coconut

½ cup currants or golden raisins (optional)

1 cup chopped pecans, walnuts, or almonds (optional)

1 teaspoon salt

4 teaspoons baking powder

1 teaspoon cinnamon

½ teaspoon nutmeg

¼ teaspoon ground cloves (optional)

1 teaspoon vanilla extract

5 tablespoons olive oil

INSTRUCTIONS

Preheat oven to 350°F.

In a large mixing bowl, beat eggs until creamy with an electric mixer. Add rest of ingredients to eggs and blend. Batter will be thick.

Grease 9x13-inch glass baking dish with coconut oil (or use cooking spray). Spread batter in baking dish and bake for 45-50 minutes.

Cool, cut into 18-24 pieces. The bars freeze nicely for a grab-and-go breakfast.

PEOPLE SERVED: 18-24

ETCETERA

My brother-in-law turned me on to this recipe. It's really easy to make and I don't get hungry before lunch.

The funny thing is our dog, Shadow, really likes them too.

She always begs to have some.

She likes the smoothie more than her favorite treats.

DANA SIMPSON

BLUEBERRY SMOOTHIE RECIPE
WITH WILDROOTS FLAX SEED

INGREDIENTS

1 scant cup non-fat milk

¼ cup low fat organic yogurt

2 tablespoons 50% Manitoba Harvest Hemp protein powder

2 tablespoons WildRoots golden flax seed

1 ⅓ cups frozen organic blueberries

1 organic banana

1 tablespoon Udo's oil

INSTRUCTIONS

Place all ingredients in a blender and blend until smooth.

PEOPLE SERVED: 2

I have always had a weakness for gourmet cinnamon rolls. If I had to choose two foods to live off of for the rest of my life, it would be pizza and cinnamon rolls!

My daughter, Kaitlyn, and I have made a tradition of making these cinnamon rolls the night before major holidays. We slow proof them in the refrigerator so that they can be baked off when we wake up on the holiday.

MARK DAVIDSON

AWARD-WINNING GOURMET CINNAMON ROLLS

INGREDIENTS

Dough:

3 cups all-purpose flour

1 package active dry yeast

¼ cup sugar

1 ½ teaspoons salt

1 egg, beaten

1 cup milk, warm

¼ cup shortening

Cinnamon Filling:

½ stick (2 ounce) salted butter, melted

½ cup brown sugar, packed

¼ cup granulated sugar

1 teaspoon all-purpose flour

1 tablespoon ground cinnamon

Glaze:

2 cups powdered sugar

1 teaspoon vanilla

2 tablespoons butter, melted

2 tablespoons milk

INSTRUCTIONS

Add 2 cups flour and dry yeast together in a large bowl and blend thoroughly. Add sugar, egg, salt, shortening, and warm milk (less than 110°F.). Mix with your favorite wooden spoon until a smooth batter is formed. While stirring, begin adding an additional cup of flour until a stiff dough forms. Turn dough out onto a well-floured cutting board and begin kneading for about 10 minutes or until the dough is velvety and smooth. Place dough in a large greased bowl covered with plastic wrap or a tea towel. Allow the dough to double in size (ferment) in a warm place. "Punch" the dough to release the gas produced by the yeast fermenting.

While dough is fermenting, prepare the cinnamon filling by incorporating the melted butter, sugars, cinnamon and flour together until well blended. Set aside. Turn dough out onto a floured cutting board. Roll dough into a rectangle (about 14 x 12 inches). Spread the cinnamon filling over the dough sheet, but leave a 1 inch strip along one of the longer ends. At the opposite end, start rolling up the dough, jelly-roll style. Brush a small amount of water on bare edge and pinch the dough together to help seal the log.

Cut the 14 inch log in half then each can be cut in half so you end up with 4 small logs. These small logs are cut into 3 equal sized rolls. Place 12 rolls in a 9x13-inch greased pan. Cover rolls with a tea towel and proof in a warm area until doubled in size. Bake in a preheated 375°F. oven for around 20 minutes or until golden brown.

Make up glaze. Add powdered sugar to a bowl and slowly mixing in the melted butter, vanilla and milk with a large fork until a creamy icing is formed. Drizzle icing over hot rolls.

Alternate proofing method for hot out of the oven roll in the early morning: Instead of placing the rolls to proof in a warm spot, place the covered pan in the refrigerator for a slow proofing. I like to allow the roll to proof halfway before placing them in the refrigerator. When you wake up in the morning, remove rolls from refrigerator and place in a warm spot for 15-30 minutes before baking.

PEOPLE SERVED: 12 SERVINGS

My grandmother lived with us when I was growing up and is, without a doubt, the reason why I chose baking as a profession and ultimately found my way here to CM. She baked everything from scratch – from bread to cookies to pancakes – and left a treasure of handwritten notes and recipes in her well-used cookbooks that my sister and I have and use today. One of my prized possessions is the 3x5 notecard with the original cherry coffee cake recipe in her handwriting.

This is my all-time favorite recipe and my ultimate go-to comfort food. Whenever I bake this coffee cake **I think of my grandmother and the influence she had on my life.** I have no doubt that she would be proud of where I am today.

I hope that you enjoy Grandma's Cherry Coffee Cake as much as I do.

Love you Grandma!

DAWN FRYDENLUND

GRANDMA'S CHERRY COFFEE CAKE

INGREDIENTS

Streusel Topping:

¼ cup butter, softened

¼ cup brown sugar, packed

⅓ cup granulated sugar

⅓ cup all-purpose flour

1 teaspoon cinnamon

Coffee Cake:

1 egg

¾ cup granulated sugar

⅓ cup butter, melted

½ cup milk

1 teaspoon vanilla

1 ½ cups all-purpose flour

2 ½ teaspoons baking powder, leveled

½ teaspoon salt, leveled

1 can (~21 ounce) cherry pie filling, use all fruit leaving ~⅓ cup of the filling liquid

INSTRUCTIONS

Preheat oven to 350°F.

For the streusel topping, combine the softened butter, brown sugar, granulated sugar, flour, and cinnamon in a bowl. Blend with a fork until mixture is crumbled together.

Set aside while preparing the coffee cake batter.

For the coffee cake, beat the egg in a large bowl with an electric hand mixer until frothy. Add the sugar and melted butter to the bowl and continue blending with the mixer for ~1 minute.

Using a spatula, stir in the milk and vanilla by hand, incorporating well. Gently blend in the flour, baking powder and salt, stirring until combined.

Pour batter into a greased 8x8-inch pan and spread evenly to edges. Top with cherries and spread evenly. Sprinkle generously with the streusel topping, reserving ~⅓ cup to sprinkle on after baking.

Bake coffee cake for 35 – 40 minutes. Use a toothpick (or clean knife) to insert in center of the cake to check for doneness.

Remove from the oven and sprinkle on remaining streusel topping. Allow to cool 10 – 15 minutes before cutting and serving.

Tastes best when eaten warm!

PEOPLE SERVED: 8 - 10

DESSERTS

My mom was raised on a farm in a little slice of Montana heaven called Eden. As an adult, she moved in to the closest big town, Great Falls, and raised 6 kids. **We got to visit the farm every Sunday.**

While growing up, I remember my grandpa driving in from the farm with fresh eggs and cream to sell.

My mom always got several dozen fresh eggs and a quart jar of sour cream. She would put the fresh cream in the fridge and leave half of it until it was good and sour and ready for use in our all-time favorite desserts – Sour Cream Chocolate Cake and Sour Cream Donuts. Both of these recipes came from our Norwegian neighbor and lifelong friend, Orpha Fossum. The cake is dense, delicious and has a wonderful hot drizzled chocolate frosting on top. **Mouth wateringly good to the last bite!**

To this day, when I make either of these recipes, I remember the joy of having that farm and the goodness we shared with our big family and neighbors when grandpa came to town.

RAYE RAPP

ORPHA'S SOUR CREAM DONUTS

INGREDIENTS

½ cup sour cream
(use good, heavy whipping cream and sour with vinegar)

½ cup sour milk

2 eggs, beaten

1 teaspoon vanilla

1 teaspoon nutmeg

1 cup sugar

1 teaspoon baking soda

1 teaspoon baking powder

3 cups flour

INSTRUCTIONS

Combine all the ingredients.

Roll out the dough onto a floured board. Use a rolling pin to spread the dough to about ¼ or ½ inch thickness, lightly flouring as you go along if the pin sticks.

Use a donut cutter or a small round glass to cut out the round donuts. Drop into hot shortening in a deep fryer set at 375°F.

Cook about 4 minutes total, 2 on each side. Use a slotted spoon to flip the donut. Remove the donuts using the slotted spoon and set them on a plate lined with paper towels.

Place a paper towel over the top of the donuts to soak up the grease on top as well as the bottom. You can also flip the donuts occasionally with fresh paper towels to remove more grease.

ADDITIONAL NOTES

Look for good, heavy cream at specialty stores (Costco) for use in this recipe. You may need to sour the cream with vinegar.

PEOPLE SERVED: 24 DONUTS

ETCETERA

"Forever my friend, forever my love..."
Ray Lamontagne

Not only is my husband the greatest man who ever walked the face of the earth, but he is also an amazing artist, a talented musician, an incredible cook, and a lovable people person. He makes friends easily and loves to entertain them at our Moose Lodge by playing music, jamming, or just making people smile by whipping up something yummy in the kitchen. One thing that he loves to make for our guests are these pudding shots.

These amazing pudding shots are crowd pleasers *(especially on a hot summer night).* Your guests will love them.

Enjoy!

YOLANDE LYONS

BANANA & COCONUT PUDDING SHOTS

INGREDIENTS

1 package (approximately 3.5 ounces) of instant banana pudding mix

¾ cup milk

¾ cup coconut rum

1 tub (approximately 8 ounces) of whipped cream

INSTRUCTIONS

Mix pudding and milk until well blended.

Add rum, mix well. Fold in whipped cream.

Divide into individual servings.

Keep in freezer.

ADDITIONAL NOTES

Variations: Try using chocolate pudding mix and coffee liquor! Experiment with different pudding and alcohol flavors or try folding things in...like crushed Oreo cookies or chocolate chips.

PEOPLE SERVED: 20

ACKNOWLEDGEMENTS

We want to thank the **MANY** volunteers that made this **AMAZING** cookbook possible!

COOKBOOK TEAM:
- Shelley Vanderpoel
- Dana Ross
- Val Thorson
- Bob Wallach

SHAREPOINT GURU:
- Bobbi Miller

SITE CHEERLEADERS:
- Tiffany Luby
- Krista Heys
- Brett Allison
- Heather Davis
- Val Thorson

POTLUCK CREWS:
- Claudia Strong
- Jean Green
- Rachyl Miller
- Maggie Liming
- Sandra Bensley
- Erin Burdick
- Yolande Lyons
- Tami Taylor
- Melissa Nichols
- Lori Vilkanskas

PROOFREADERS:
- Shelley Vanderpoel
- Dana Ross
- Val Thorson
- Rachyl Miller

RECIPE SAMPLERS:
- Raye Rapp
- Yolande Lyons
- Erin Burdick
- Joann Green
- Sandra Bensley
- Jean Green
- Claudia Strong
- Tammy Barr
- Sue Engdahl-Shaver
- Lavanya Venkateswar
- Shelley Vanderpoel
- Naomi McKay
- Judy Else

BOOK ORDERING:
- Gail Hopkins

CONTRIBUTORS:

As seen in the book….**thank you** for your great recipes and stories!

CONVERSION TABLE

LIQUID MEASURES

1 Cup	8 Fluid Ounces	1/2 Pint	237 ml
2 Cups	16 Fluid Ounces	1 Pint	474 ml
4 Cups	32 Fluid Ounces	1 Quart	946 ml
2 Pints	32 Fluid Ounces	1 Quart	0.964 liters
4 Quarts	128 Fluid Ounces	1 Gallon	3.784 liters
8 Quarts	One Peck		
4 Pecks	One Bushel		
Dash	Less Than 1/4 Teaspoon		

DRY MEASURES

3 Teaspoons	1 Tablespoon	1/2 Ounce	14.3 Grams	
2 Tablespoons	1/8 Cup	1 Fluid Ounce	28.3 Grams	
4 Tablespoons	1/4 Cup	2 Fluid Ounces	56.7 Grams	
5 1/3 Tablespoons	1/3 Cup	2.6 Fluid Ounces	75.6 Grams	
8 Tablespoons	1/2 Cup	4 Ounces	113.4 Grams	1 Stick Butter
12 Tablespoons	3/4 Cup	6 Ounces	.375 Pound	170 Grams
32 Tablespoons	2 Cups	16 Ounces	1 Pound	453.6 Grams
64 Tablespoons	4 Cups	32 Ounces	2 Pounds	907 Grams

TEMPERATURE

CELSIUS	»	FAHRENHEIT
125		257
130		266
135		275
140		284
145		293
150		302
155		311
160		320
165		329
170		338
175		347
180		356
185		365
190		374
195		383
200		392
205		401
210		410
215		419
220		428
225		437
230		446
235		455
240		464
245		473
250		482
255		491
260		500

FAHRENHEIT	»	CELSIUS
270		132
280		138
290		143
300		149
310		154
320		160
330		166
340		171
350		177
360		182
370		188
380		193
390		199
400		204
410		210
420		216
430		221
440		227
450		232
460		238
470		243
480		249
490		254
500		260
510		266
520		271
530		277
540		282